A Broad River

BRATHAY HALL TRUST

D1386482

Francis Scott.

A Broad River

BRATHAY HALL TRUST

50 YEARS *of* PROGRESS

MAURICE DYBECK

CONTENTS

Published 1996
Brathay Hall Trust,
Ambleside, Cumbria
LA22 0HP

© *Brathay Hall Trust*
ISBN 0 9529200 0 X

Designed by
Cooper Design Group,
Penrith

Printed in England by
Philip Myers Press
(Holdings) Ltd, Warrington

FOREWORD

For two centuries, the plain but elegant face of Brathay Hall has looked south across its peaceful parkland to Lake Windermere. Lakeland rains, snows, winds and sunshine have mellowed this once 'white palace' to soft grey. Now it fits as naturally into the landscape as does the fell behind it.

For the past 50 years, the Brathay Hall Trust has used this lovely house and its estate to provide experiences that so many people remember all their lives. In 1940, while England held its breath during the darkest days of the evacuation from Dunkirk, a group of youth leaders came together at Brathay. Over that memorable weekend of still and sunlit weather, those men planned with hope and astonishing certainty how Francis Scott's benefaction could best help the nation's youth once the war was over.

Thus, vision and philanthropy became reality. Brathay's early work of 'Holidays with Purpose', packed into seven days that mix of activities in the mountains and on the lake, in drama and in art, which later became such a distinctive feature of the month-long courses. Walking and camping in the fells, painting pictures and acting, were all used as equally important vehicles to challenge, stretch and grow the young men from industry who came to Brathay.

Later, the scientific expeditions to measure the previously uncharted depths of the Lakeland tarns became the Brathay Exploration Group. In any one year its expeditions could stretch from Norway to North Africa and from the Lake District to Uganda. The leaders could be geography teachers, university students or young industrialists. The expedition members would be sixth-formers from private and grammar schools, and apprentices who had already done a Brathay course.

Later still, the interest and enthusiasm of those volunteers in the Exploration Group triggered the establishment of the Brathay Field Study Centre.

And so, some 25 years after its foundation, Brathay had three distinct but complementary strands: at the Hall were the month-long courses, by then for both young men and women from industry and commerce; Old Brathay was the base for field studies, providing courses for A-level students and undergraduates; and in the woods on the estate was the headquarters of the Brathay Exploration Group.

Gradually the courses at the Hall evolved. Companies were soon no longer prepared to send their young employees away for a month, and two to three weeks became the norm. At the same time, Brathay persuaded clients to use this type of training for managers as well. This became the springboard for the Brathay of today, where development training for young people and for managers has taken centre stage.

For 40 years, Francis Scott's family trust provided Brathay with an annual subsidy. This funded the youth work, whose sponsors were never able to pay an economic fee. When that regular subvention finally ceased, Brathay faced the challenge of finding other ways to subsidise the youth work, and management training seemed the obvious answer. This field is an intensely competitive market, but by delivering a first class service, it has been possible to create a surplus, which is used to subsidise the work for youth. Maintaining a balance between management work and youth work, and generating a surplus is a business challenge of no mean size, but the skills needed in one area are relevant to the others, and each adds value to the whole.

Over the years, Brathay has made a very particular contribution to outdoor education and training in several ways. As a single centre that was generously funded for many years, it has been able to follow an independent course. Physical endeavour has never been the dominant activity; the worlds of the intellect and the spirit are key elements in Brathay's work. Above all, the emphasis has always been on development of each person as an individual.

Brathay is an intensely human place that allows people to change because they see the sense of it for themselves and not because any system tells them to. This is the reason that so many who have known Brathay as course members, as staff, as voluntary leaders or as governors and trustees find that it never lets them go. I am one such. My own enthusiasm and admiration for this work of national value, to which so many have contributed so much over these 50 years, is undiminished.

And why does all this matter? Because the work of Brathay is as relevant today as it has ever been. Young men and women, whoever they may be and whatever their background, need to know themselves and others better. Experience of success and understanding of failure, the growth of self-confidence together with a readiness to help the other person, are fundamental in helping people to build a fulfilled and useful life. Managers need to lead people better, to work more effectively with teams and to be enabled to open all those gates that release the real potential of those accountable to them.

It is to these issues that the work of Brathay is addressed. You, the reader of this book, will be the judge of that endeavour.

Mark Wolfson MP
Chairman of the Brathay Trustees
Westminster, August 1996

PREFACE

Brathay is a complex place and so its history is also complex. It is a 'broad river' along which much is flowing. To make things easier for the reader, this book has been designed to serve different needs. Although most of it is in chronological order, it has been divided into 10 main themes, so that it is possible to go straight to a theme of interest without reading all the rest. For those who want to check on the chronology, there is a calendar of key events in the appendices, as well as details of what goes on in a typical week. For particular names or events, refer to the index.

The initial research for this book, some of the interviews and the writing of the first draft were the work of Alan Hankinson, and the trustees are grateful for this useful foundation for the final book. Many people – too many to list – have been most helpful in giving information about Brathay, their perceptions of what it has achieved and, in many cases, what it has done for them personally. Former principals and members of staff have given freely of their time and produced much documentary evidence both on the work at Brathay and on the contemporary scene.

Despite all the added pressures of the 50th Anniversary celebrations, Audrey Hallowell, with her usual calm competence, has organised the typing and production of this book. Brathay is grateful to her.

Lastly, a word of thanks to my fellow trustees. Their scrutiny has been firm but supportive, and I only hope that the finished product lives up to the high standards set by Brathay in everything it does.

Maurice Dybeck
Ambleside
August 1996

SETTING THE SCENE

FIFTY YEARS OF GROWTH

Brathay's approach to people has always been rather special. Its founder, Francis Scott, always believed in doing things well, as his highly successful life in business demonstrated. He carried that philosophy into his work with young people, in boys' clubs in the 1930s, in the wartime Boy Leader training courses which he encouraged, and in the foundation of the Brathay Hall Trust in 1946, dedicated to the betterment of young people. Thanks to Scott's generosity, Brathay was not constrained by having to provide courses that were financially viable from day one. As any pioneer in any field of endeavour knows, new ideas need time to take root and be accepted, and many good ideas can be lost by the need to make ends meet.

This book aims to describe how Brathay's ideas came into being and how they developed. Not all ideas survive to this day, but in an evolving organisation one would not expect them to. Ideas fall by the wayside when they are no longer relevant, when they become too expensive, or when they have been copied by others who now do them rather better. Despite its charge to help young people, at times even Brathay has been unable to afford to do the very work it first set out to do. Scott's largesse was not limitless and, over the years, Brathay has rightly had to adjust to the fact that however good a product may be, someone has to pay for it, and it is best if that burden is shared according to the ability to pay.

Brathay's work in all its diversity is celebrated in these pages. It is important to recognise that the ups and downs in Brathay's contribution to youth work have been largely a response to the ups and downs of economic opportunity. Put simply, if firms can no longer afford to send young workers on a four-week course, four-week courses cannot be run; and if Brathay is constrained to charge the full rate for Field Study courses for students, universally regarded as very successful, such courses must decline.

Many of Brathay's successful courses with 'inner city' youngsters and those with social problems, have only been made possible by generous financial support from trusts such as the Rank Foundation, corporate sponsors and charitable foundations. There was a time, a decade or so ago, when a lot of government money was available for specialist youth training courses, as a palliative for youth unemployment. Opportunities come and go and the skill of Brathay management has to be in seizing the right opportunities and developing them. Alone, Brathay can offer its experience to no more than a fraction of young people, but it *can* stand as a 'powerhouse of ideas' that can drive others into action.

BRATHAY TODAY

Before we begin at the beginning, it is useful to consider what Brathay has become, and the examples that follow illustrate something of the diversity of the activities there today. To an outsider, the common theme may not be apparent, and all these short courses may seem to have little connection with the four-week courses that began almost 50 years ago. But someone who had attended one of those early courses would see much that was familiar, especially the direct interest of staff in every member of the course and the concern that every member should understand what the course is about and that he or she should use the experience of Brathay in a way appropriate to his or her needs.

The team from Rover

It looked as if take-off of the new aircraft was going to be one and a half hours late. But in this simulation, every hour was a month, and that made it serious. Simulation or not, the members of this team from the Design Department of Rover were determined to make up any lost time and end up with a success. These people were used to challenge and Brathay had given them a big one. The fact that it included making a 5m wingspan aeroplane, 'flying' it, dropping 'bombs', and also making a promotional video on the theme 'On Target', and all in 24 hours, was incidental. The real challenge for these 14 people aged between 20 and 50+, was to demonstrate that they could, through four days of demanding exercises, achieve certain objectives. These objectives, set by Brathay in partnership with the firm, related to working together effectively. Every course has its own objectives and these were the ones for the team from Rover in April 1996.

By the end of the event delegates will have:

- understood the advantages of flexible and adaptable ways of working
- built relationships across the Product Design Team
- experienced the 'power' of the team through maximisation of each individual's contribution and the utilisation of each individual's strengths
- built on strengths, rather than concentrating on weaknesses
- acknowledged the creative tension present between stylists and engineers and developed strategies for using the relationship in a positive constructive manner
- developed increased trust in colleagues and understood the advantages of developing trust within workplace teams.

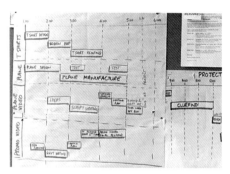

Between the rain showers, the plane was taking shape in the Brathay stableyard. They had to build an early-type biplane out of canes, string, boxes, polystyrene, wallpaper and paint. Simultaneously, others in the team had to be preparing, scripting and shooting a five-minute production that would include not only the plane, but also a series of acted sketches to demonstrate such 'on target' qualities as loyalty, planning, communication, teamwork, friendship, honesty, leadership, having the right ingredients, trust and support.

It was a bit like high class charades, since for each quality they had to prepare real and convincing 'props'. For instance, 'the right ingredients' were demonstrated by filming people mixing paint and making logos for their T-shirts (appropriately based on Rodin's *Thinker*), and 'teamwork' was demonstrated by the whole team wearing those T-shirts, leaping in the air and

shouting 'A CLASS ACT!'. 'Planning' was shown, rather predictably, by someone standing in front of wall charts, 'loyalty' got the reverse treatment with someone getting stabbed in the back, and 'support' involved borrowing some female undergarments.

In the review afterwards, they all admitted that they had had fun, whilst being conscious throughout of a serious purpose: to work effectively together. They thought that they had had clear goals, a well defined task, and a firm deadline for completion. It was a complex exercise (perhaps well beyond the competence of lesser groups), but they had welcomed that. Indeed, they said that had it been an easy exercise, achievable within, say, eight hours, they would probably have taken it in their stride and accomplished very little. As it was, the high demands gave them a buzz and they all wanted it to work to show Brathay and each other that they could do it.

Was this just like work? Some said not, since Brathay gave them clear goals, whereas things were much more diffuse at work: people moved the goalposts, changed the rules, and sometimes didn't even accept the thing you had worked so hard on. The two Brathay trainers, Godfrey and Annie, didn't take sides. Throughout the course they, too, changed the rules and moved the goalposts every now and then, just to add reality. For his aeroplane scene, Pete wanted three 'bombs' and four smoke canisters. He was only allowed one of each. The plane builders wanted more sticky tape. But supplies were limited and participants had to manage with the existing resources. The leaders asked for guidance, and the instructions were deliberately unclear. These obstacles are the stuff of all industrial life. But at Brathay, this Rover team did not perceive them as stumbling blocks, simply as problems to be solved, situations to be adapted to and – the key thought – challenges to be overcome. They had built up a momentum and nothing was going to stop them.

So, in fact, it *was* like work at Brathay, with the difference that in this setting at the end of the project you could stand back and analyse what had gone right and what had gone wrong. If there had been delays, there was no blaming someone else in another department. The finger pointed to someone in the room and this meant that there was a clear compulsion to finish the task you had put so much into. As Ken said in the review:

The deadlines seemed to be getting nearer and nearer. You then looked at what you'd produced so far, thinking 'not gonna get it done'. Then I'd think we've got so far, and that spurred you on. We hadn't stopped for hours, had we? We were starting to get a bit tired. But the fact that we'd got so far, we wanted it completed now. Everybody wanted it to succeed.

Through this project and some others in the first three days, the Brathay course had given them a chance to live out a work scenario, not in their boxed-in drawing office with artificial light and forced ventilation, but in the woods, lakes and hills of the Lake District. The projects enabled them to examine their roles in a controlled situation, and then to draw conclusions that they could take back to the workplace.

After four very full days, the last morning's review showed that the team members had made many decisions, some hopeful, some painful, about the future. What now? Their trainers said, 'Well, there's a nice coffee shop two miles up the valley. Let's meet there at 11'. No, this wasn't some joke, simply a rather civilised way of encouraging a wider reflection, amidst beautiful surroundings, on the deeper implications of what could well have been the life-changing experiences of the previous four days. *Now* we can go and build that car! And it *will* be *a class act!*

The Garstang Youth Project

There was this noise coming from the bushes in front of Brathay Hall. Then some raucous laughter and what some might call a song. I went over. It was a very large rhododendron and they were actually inside it, huddled together and full of merriment. 'Do you want to hear our song?' they asked. 'OK, go on then.' So these six young schoolgirls from a Lancashire comprehensive proceeded to regale me with their latest achievement on this busy weekend experience.

We are the Doobies, we are the best,
We're much better than all the rest.

We went on the ropes, and did it well,
Together we are, really swell.

We went in the ghyll, we got real wet.
We're dried out now, so don't be upset.

Back at Eagle Crag, Ann Hall, the Brathay trainer who was running the course, asked them what they were getting out of it. It was not a formal session and out came a lively ragbag of responses:

It was really challenging this time. [They'd been once before last autumn.] *I found the ropes really hard. Cos you've got a fear of heights, haven't you?*

We've mixed with people we wouldn't have mixed with at school...

We can work as a team and help each other, and comfort each other.

We was supporting them ...
We can work really well as a team if we put our minds to it.

That's one thing we've learned: you've gotta listen to other people, like.

You've gotta treat people the way you want them to treat you. It's not just you, you, you; it's all of you.
You've gotta support them, and stuff like that.

Despite the high spirits, this was not a fun weekend. Its formal description was Personal and Social Education (PSE) using a Partnership between School, the Youth Service and Brathay staff. It was part of a progressive programme that started and finished in the school and in which Brathay was a vital element. Although the nature of the course was fairly new, the ideas behind it – personal development of young people – go back to the very beginnings of Brathay and the stimulus of its founder.

The MANWEB (Merseyside and North Wales Electricity Board) course

'Don't forget to buckle back everything twice and then we'll check your harnesses to make sure everything's OK. If you take your harness off at any time during the day come back to us and ask us to re-check it.'

There was a mixture of curiosity and apprehension as the group looked into the tree-lined rocky hollow ahead. It wouldn't be difficult at first, if you didn't mind getting wet, but then, of course, most people did. So you had to hop from rock to rock, skirt the pools and scramble past the waterfalls.

The day's tasks for this group of apprentices (seven men and one woman) began with a ghyll scramble from New Dungeon Ghyll some 1100ft up to Stickle Tarn. At the start the apprentices had put on safety harnesses and the trainer's role was pure instruction. Now was the time for some advice on helping others: 'Steve, if you need to grip someone else, remember people's hands can be rather sweaty. It's best if you hold people like this: by the wrist.'

The going got harder and, over one tricky bit, Jane fell and cut her leg. Perhaps the others had not been helping her as much as she had expected. But how much help did she expect? The others were trying to be 'politically correct' and so not giving her any special favours just because she was female. Maybe they were leaning too far the other way. There was a short pause while the first aid kit was produced and a plaster applied, by the other members of the team.

There were bits of the scramble where it was essential to help each other and this was what made the exercise so valuable. Having told them how to help each other, the trainer left it to them to decide when to offer each other assistance. It didn't always work out right, however, so at the next break, after asking, 'Anybody finding it difficult?' and, equally important, 'Are you enjoying it?', one trainer trotted out a lecture:

One thing I noticed a couple of times, when you get over a difficult bit, you tend to shoot on, rather than thinking 'I found it difficult so perhaps the person behind me also might'. So be aware of this on the next bit and if you find it tricky, the likelihood of the person behind you also finding it tricky is quite strong. So give each other a hand and point out the difficult bits.

Like Field Marshall Montgomery, he told them the vital message twice; and that message could be applied to more than scrambling up waterfalls.

The lunch-break was at Stickle Tarn, and they were all flaked out. Now came discussion of the task for the afternoon. Ahead of them, across the cliff face of Pavey Ark, lay Jack's Rake, an exposed scramble with a few tricky bits in the middle.

'It'll probably take us about an hour and a half to go up it and then back to this point, for the descent. We don't always do this bit but you're moving well as a group and you're all capable of getting there,' one trainer said.

Clearly the prospect overawed some of them, and the trainers encouraged them to say how they felt about it. 'This is about putting yourselves into the stretch zone,' they were told. One was ready and waiting, 'I don't think I've achieved anything yet today...'. Another, proud but tired, said, 'I've achieved a lot'. Someone else, thinking that enough is enough, tried to turn thoughts homewards, 'How long will it take us to get back down?'

Then one of the members made a suggestion, 'Why not whoever wants to go up...?' He tried a bit of sounding out for allies, 'Do you want to go up, Mac? Say if you do.' Mac said, 'I'm not bothered,' perhaps waiting to see which way the voting would go. Trainers did their best to see that things were not swayed by the stronger personalities. 'It's up to each one of you to give your

honest opinion,' they said. Sensing the non-committal nature of rather too many of the group, Matthew stormed in with, 'I thought we were meant to be acting as a bit of a team, like, not all "I wanna do this" or "I can't be bothered".' Jane retorted, 'But there's no point in someone saying they· don't wanna go and everybody having to go is there? We wanna find out how many people want to go and how many don't!' Tom tried to cool it, 'All the same, you can go through life saying "can't be bothered to do this and that". People have got to push you, haven't they?' But there was opposition to this view. 'On the other hand, at the end of the day, I've been pushed enough up here and I reckon that's far enough.' And another said, 'Well said John! If they want to go, I don't see why I should have to go'.

The daunting task of pulling together this fiery dialogue fell to the trainer. But she was not going to absolve them from any responsibility.

'It's very much up to you how much you want to push yourselves. This ascent would certainly be a good challenge,' she said. 'What will happen to us if we don't decide to come up?' said one anxious voice.

'Nothing. But you will have to live with your decision. You live with the consequences of that decision. And staying here might well be the right decision for you.'

Since the route was a circular one returning to the lunch point, it was possible to split the party so that five could make the ascent while the others waited for them to return. Both halves were conscious that they were going to live with their decision; the ones who waited by the tarn were rather subdued. And the others? The triumphant photos taken on the top half an hour later said it all.

Despite the occasional nonchalance, it had been a demanding day for all of them. It was just one small part of a totally new experience provided by this five-day development training course. The rest of the programme was a mixture of indoor and outdoor tasks, discussions, and meetings, each one very different but all leading to the same clear objectives for this particular course: confidence, interpersonal skills, responsibility at work, and citizenship.

The youngsters from Anglesey

At 9 a.m. they were gathering in the barn to begin the day's work. Around the room there were display boards on which, the evening before, each of the participants had pinned their background stories, their 'life maps'. They made depressing reading: tales of persistent truancy and broken family homes, sickness and accidents, drugs and failed relationships, an all-pervading feeling of having been let down by life, of loneliness, hopelessness and joblessness. They had been asked to state their prevailing fears and it was a sad list: heights, failure, being alone, crowds, public-speaking, the dark, and, most frequently, not getting a job. They were also asked what it was they were hoping to get out of the course. The replies were varied: 'to get more confidence', 'to do everything on the course', 'to gain something in my life', 'to get qualifications'; but they were unanimous in their hope that it would help them 'to get a job'.

The group comprised 10 unemployed young people from the Holyhead region of Anglesey, north Wales. Not thrusting successful professionals bouncing with confidence like some of the Brathay clientele, but adolescents and young adults who had had a tough and discouraging deal out of their lives so far. Their needs were many: self-respect, confidence, wider interests, encouragement, more stable relationships, and jobs.

On management courses, the training staff can afford to be demanding, sometimes even difficult, because they know the participants can take it. The treatment of these young people from Holyhead had to be much more gentle and sympathetic. Brian Woof, in charge of their training, was quiet and understanding.

The youngsters had all volunteered for a 12-week course organised by the Prince's Trust Volunteers, an organisation set up under the inspiration of the Prince of Wales to help young disadvantaged people get more involved with the community around them (see Theme 6). Coincidentally, this course was being subsidised by MANWEB, and one of its young training officers, Terry Jones, was with them. He was in charge of them for the whole 12 weeks and had already spent an introductory week with them in Wales, allowing them all to get to know each other, trying to mould them into an effective team, and preparing them for the three months ahead. They had come to Brathay for four and a half days, and the aims of the programme were:

- for young people of different backgrounds to work together
- to build a team to work together for the next 10 weeks of the programme
- to develop self-awareness, self-esteem and self-confidence in individuals
- to establish a way of working that includes reviewing and self-assessment.

The group was accommodated in Old Brathay, an 18th century house that had just been completely refurbished. It was clean, convenient and basic. They slept in four-bunk bedrooms, and there were facilities for cooking and communal eating. To help build up the team spirit, they were catering for themselves and seemed to be enjoying it. They had done their own shopping and worked out duty rosters for cooking, cleaning, washing up duties, and so on.

One by one, Woof got them to stand up alongside their 'life map' and talk the group through it,

expanding on key points and answering his gentle but probing questions when it was not quite clear what they were trying to say. Many of them were so tentative and shy that it was hard to hear them. But they were being remarkably serious, honest and frank. One teenage boy, whose life story showed that he had never been able to stick at anything for long, said that his greatest fear was that he might not be able to last the course. Another boy's chief ambition was to give up smoking. One young woman in her early 20s described the collapse of her too-early marriage. Another said she felt let down and lonely. In his questioning, Woof tried all the time to encourage them towards a more positive view of their situation. The message was that they had to look quietly and thoughtfully at their lives and realise that there were ways of improving themselves and strengthening their attitudes. There were also ways in which members of the group could help and strengthen each other.

For the next morning session they all trooped down to the boathouse to learn how to manage rowing boats, the big Brathay whalers. There were staff technicians there to teach them how to put on lifejackets, the correct procedure for lowering the boats into the water, and then how to get on board, five to a boat – four to row and one to steer, shout the orders and keep time. Once afloat there was considerable initial confusion with much shouting and the boats going in all directions. But they soon got the hang of it and began to operate in unison.

Jones, the man from MANWEB, said that working with them was not easy. The kids could be difficult and some of them were disturbed and hard to handle at times. In this group the girls were already complaining that two of the lads in the next room had kept them awake last night, drinking beer and talking very loudly. This would have to be sorted out soon, although he thought that the girls would manage to do it for themselves. Most of them were already beginning to think and feel as members of a team and to enjoy all the new experiences in this unfamiliar environment. If the work was sometimes frustrating, it was also fascinating. After this Brathay experience, which he thought was invaluable, the youngsters would embark on a Community Project that they had come up with to turn a bit of wasteland in Holyhead into a small park for elderly folk in the area. At the end of their 12-week course, they would all get a 'Profile of Achievement' certificate, which would help them into further education or in their search for jobs.

The change wrought in them during their short time at Brathay was remarkable. By the end they were really working as a team, listening to each other's suggestions and discussing ideas in a

cool rational manner. They were altogether more relaxed, more confident and more enthusiastic. They were all wearing T-shirts inscribed with the letters P.T.V. (Prince's Trust Volunteers), which they had designed and screen-printed themselves, in the Brathay studio.

One of the tasks for the group while at Brathay was to produce a show to put on on the final night. When it began, each of them introduced themselves and made a brief statement about what they had done at Brathay and what they had learned. They demonstrated their skills at fitting safety harnesses, and spoke of their pride in the fact that everyone in the group had got round the ropes course. They had enjoyed everything, especially the ghyll scrambling, clawing their way up a steep gully and getting wet through in the process. They had gained courage and confidence, they said. Their style of presentation, in sharp contrast to their manner only a few days before, certainly confirmed this. After the show, they adjourned to the dining room for a farewell meal, this time not cooked by themselves and accompanied by wine.

TWO STREAMS: THE ORIGINS OF DEVELOPMENT TRAINING

Despite the diversity of courses, there are two main streams running through the activities at Brathay: Outdoor Management Development (OMD) and Personal and Social Development for Young People. Despite their apparently different aims, these streams share a common source: the time-honoured, personal, Brathay approach known now as 'development training'. The OMD story has been one of steady success. It is a field pioneered by Brathay in 1969, and many have followed since. Indeed, there are now so many people fishing the waters of OMD that today you need to have not only quality but also a strong marketing department if you are to land the right catch.

Development training is about learning by doing, and there is a full description of how it is used by Brathay at the start of Theme 7. The following account of its origins is adapted from *The History of Development Training* by Dr Bertie Everard.

The deepest roots of development training go back to pre-Christian times. The concept of 'whole person development' can be ascribed to Plato who, in the 4th century BC described education as 'the simultaneous and harmonious development of all aspects of the human personality'. He also called it 'cleaning up the sour pastures of youth', which is recognisable as one modern application of development training. The concept of self-discovery also has classical origins, from the phrase 'know thyself', to the Greek attitude to games, which exemplified the link between physical activity and personal development, to the Roman motto *mens sana in corpore sano* (a healthy mind in a healthy body). Judaeo-Christian and Buddhist philosophies also advocate the notion of the whole person, and the theme of self-knowledge through hardship pervades much Christian and Eastern religious teaching. This idea is a common feature, too, of many native communities in which youths of both sexes have to undergo initiation rites. These often consist of challenging experiences, such as wilderness isolation with other adolescents, and the mastery of complex concepts and skills related to that society's culture.

The adventure component of development training is more easily traceable to the rise of the boys' movements in the late 19th and early 20th centuries, when George Williams founded the Young Men's Christian Association (YMCA, 1844), Sir William Smith founded the Boys' Brigade (1883) and Lord Baden-Powell founded the Boy Scouts (1908). The book *Scouting for Boys* presented outdoor activities as full of adventure, while the conscious development of a set of values was firmly embedded in the aims of all three movements.

A much more recent development is the use of the experiential learning cycle, with its emphasis on 'learning to learn', as a key component of development training. It is true that in the past the *concrete experience* was often followed by *reflective observation,* when participants were encouraged to write diaries of their adventurous experiences, but the stages of *abstract conceptualisation* and *active experimentation* were not firmly followed through in process reviews until industrial training influences were brought to bear on development training (at Brathay) in the late 1960s. The ingredients of novelty and variety were clearly part of the development training experiences being provided in the late 1940s, and attempts were also being made to shape the learning climate, to inspire, to develop optimism and trust, to show concern for others, to encourage and support risk, and to facilitate authentic communication.

The evolution of development training is marked by the contribution of a number of pioneers. Perhaps the best known is Kurt Hahn who founded Gordonstoun School and, with Laurence Holt, the Outward Bound Trust. No less a contribution was made independently by Scott, founder and benefactor of the Brathay Hall Trust, whose staff have long been at the leading edge of developing this style of training. Both of these trusts were well connected with progressive firms in industry, such as the steel companies and ICI. The adaptive transfer of good training practice from industry, which had in turn been influenced by that used in the armed forces for developing leaders, did much to enrich and enhance development training practice. Hahn, himself, was impressed by what he saw on a visit to Brathay, particularly the blend of the creative and the practical achieved in art and drama work.

The outdoors in management training

Scott spent heavily on training the staff in the insurance company he owned, sending them to the Management College at Ashridge. Philip Sadler, former principal of Ashridge, gives a perspective on some of the developments since those days.

Thirty years ago, 'management' was taught with blackboard and chalk in the classroom, like history or mathematics. Management colleges ran four-week or 12-week courses, and places like Outward Bound were considered rather cranky. Then people began to try various forms of experiential learning – simulation exercises, case studies, even Lego bricks, not just listening, but going out and doing things. For younger managers, the outdoors was now considered a suitable theatre.

Then, in the 1970s, leadership was seen to be important. At Ashridge, we contracted out an outdoor element for some of our courses. We came to see that sending our students away to suffer common hardships and perils made them more dependent upon each another. They were built into a team.

Current thinking in training puts the needs and welfare of the individual first. An increasing number of companies realise that this is important. New awareness of the significance of our environment is also leading people to realise that the way to safeguard the vitality of our inner cities is to put resources into the personal development of our children, rather than concentrating on mopping up oil spills.

EARLY HISTORY

BRATHAY BEFORE THE TRUST

Brathay is the name of a river that rises in the heart of Lakeland, near the Three Shires Stone high up on the Wrynose Pass. The river runs through Little Langdale Tarn and Elterwater to empty into England's biggest lake, Windermere. The name derives from the Scandinavian *breidh-a*, which meant 'broad water' to the Viking invaders who moved into these English highlands with their sheep over a thousand years ago.

For many centuries Brathay has also been the name given to the land that adjoins the north-west corner of Lake Windermere. It is an area of rolling meadowland and fine old broad-leaf trees, with views across the lake to the south and east, with Todd Crag and Loughrigg Fell immediately to the north, and the fine high ridges of Crinkle Crags and Bowfell, and the unmistakable humpy outline of the Langdale Pikes, to the west.

EARLY OWNERS OF BRATHAY HALL AND OLD BRATHAY

George Law

In the latter half of the 18th century, John Christian Curwen, an iron ore magnate from Workington, bought Belle Isle, the island in Windermere, and there built an odd circular house that the poet Wordsworth, a local lad, derided as a 'pepper pot'. In 1788 the whole Brathay estate was purchased by George Law, the son of an attorney in Ulverston. He was a local property owner and also had an interest in Backbarrow ironworks, situated beyond the south end of Windermere. Law had the old farmhouse knocked down, and in its place raised a handsome three-storey mansion faced with pale sandstone, which he named Brathay Hall. It is this building that has stood at the heart of the activities of the Brathay Hall Trust for the past 50 years.

The poet Coleridge didn't like the look of Brathay Hall at all. 'Amid these awful mountains, Mr Law has built a white palace at the head of Wynandermere...'.

The exact date of the completion of Brathay Hall is uncertain, but we know that Law, a bachelor, lived in it with his sister for only a few years before he died in 1802, aged 56.

Charles Lloyd of Old Brathay

Law had done much to improve the buildings at Old Brathay, which had once been an alehouse, and in 1799 he sold the house to Charles Lloyd. Lloyd came from a wealthy Quaker family that had made its fortune in banking in Birmingham, but his true interest was not in business but in the artistic and intellectual world. As a young man he had fallen under the spell of Samuel Taylor Coleridge, who was only three years older than himself but already making his name as a brilliant talker and writer, deep into poetry and philosophy. For a while Lloyd had lived with the Coleridge family, paying for the privilege of daily discourse with his hero. Lloyd was bright but had poor health, was mentally unstable, and was inclined to stir up trouble among his acquaintances. A novel of his, published in 1797, portrayed Coleridge (with enough truth to make it all the more hurtful) as an eccentric over-wordy thinker who lived for the most part in an opium-induced haze.

At the time he acquired Old Brathay, Lloyd had recently married and was starting his own large family, still generously subsidised by his father. For a few years the house was a very lively and hospitable place, a regular venue for the 'Lake poets', Coleridge, Wordsworth, Robert Southey and others. Lloyd's daughter, Priscilla, later married Wordsworth's brother, Christopher. One of their acquaintances was Thomas de Quincey, an early disciple of Wordsworth's. Of his first visit, he wrote:

Already on my first hasty visit to Grasmere, in 1807, I found Charles Lloyd settled with his family at Brathay, and a resident there, I believe, of some standing. It was on a wet gloomy evening, and Miss Wordsworth and I were returning from an excursion to Esthwaite Water when suddenly in the midst of blinding rain, without previous notice, she said: 'Pray let us call for a few minutes at this house...'. On that short visit I saw enough to interest me in both Charles Lloyd and his wife and, two years after, when I became myself a permanent resident in Grasmere, the connection between us became close and intimate.

De Quincey gave a vivid description of life at Old Brathay in his book *Recollections of the Lakes and the Lake Poets.*

When I first crossed Lloyd's path at the Lakes, he was in the zenith of the brief happiness that was granted to him on earth. He stood at the very centre of earthly pleasures... Old Brathay was distinguished above every other house at the head of Windermere, or within 10 miles of that neighbourhood, by the judicious assortment of its dinner parties, and the gaiety of its soirées dansantes.

But even in those days it seems that someone was keeping a wise eye on the money. De Quincey comments:

...even for the country, Old Brathay was a cheap house; but it contained everything for comfort, nothing at all for splendour. Consequently a very large part of their income was disposable for purposes of hospitality.

Dorothy Wordsworth was a regular visitor to Old Brathay. We are told in her diaries that she frequently called on her walks over Loughrigg from Grasmere.

John Harden of Brathay Hall

In 1804 this scintillating community was joined by an accomplished, although amateur, artist called John Harden and his family. He rented Brathay Hall from Law's surviving brother, Henry, and lived there for many years with his wife, Jessy, and their three sons and two daughters. Harden chose to live there for an interesting reason. He had been born in Ireland, where his father was a wealthy landowner, and had married the daughter of an Edinburgh banker. There were pulls in both directions, but he discovered that Brathay lay just half way between Edinburgh and Dublin. Jessy Harden describes their impending move in a letter dated 14 April, 1804:

We had a letter from Mr King at Ambleside yesterday with the intelligence that he had accomplished the commission we gave him of taking a house for us and has got the best one in Westmorland about half a mile from Ambleside, situated at the head of the Lake Windermere. It is one of the prettiest places I ever saw and belongs to a poor man, Mr Henry Law, who had not spirit to enjoy it. He was next heir to a very rich man who died suddenly in the West Indies, before the elegant house he was building was finished. There is a very good garden to it and as many acres as we chose to take... On the whole we are very much pleased to have got that situation being so central for our friends in Ireland and Scotland.

Like his neighbour, Lloyd, Harden was fortunate to have no money worries. The Hardens and the Lloyds were soon good friends, their children enjoyed each other's company and it was not long before the Wordsworth children became regular visitors from Grasmere. Young Hartley Coleridge also came and played with the children and made a good impression. Later, Hartley became a schoolmaster in Ambleside and taught some of the Harden children. Other visitors included the portrait painter Henry Raeburn, the painter Julius Ibbetson from Troutbeck, and a young landscape artist called John Constable. In 1806 Jessy writes that her three-year-old son is having his picture painted by Raeburn:

...but don't suppose we are so extravagant as to get his picture painted ourselves: no such thing I can assure you. Mr R. offered to do it.

The Harden family at Brathay, 1826, (reproduced by kind permission of the Abbot Hall Gallery, Kendal).

During the Constable visit, John Harden made a sketch of Constable painting a picture of Jessy.

The Lloyds left Old Brathay in 1815 and soon after that Lloyd's mind began to give way and he was committed to an asylum. But the Hardens stayed on at the Hall for a further 15 years, living lives of enviable comfort and harmony. Of Harden's attitude to young people and helping them to understand the world, Hartley Coleridge said:

He felt that in all worthy products of true genius there is milk for babes as well as meat for strong men. It is a sore error to keep good books or good pictures from children, because they cannot understand them... In another generation, the poor little wretches will not be allowed to pick flowers until they have learned botany!

Jessy recorded the family's activities in her journals: music-making reading, sewing, playing chess or backgammon, chatting quietly, drawing and painting, and entertaining the children, and Harden portrayed their cultured domestic scene in scores of pleasant sketches and watercolours. These pictures, numbering some 300 and now in the Abbot Hall Gallery in Kendal, show features that are still identifiable by modern users of Brathay.

Harden was a man who cared for and understood people. Perhaps we have in him a glimpse of what was to become, 150 years later, a key feature of development training. In her book *John Harden of Brathay Hall*, Daphne Foskett comments that Hartley Coleridge's tribute to Harden is:

... probably the clearest picture we have of Harden's character and how his essential goodness left a lasting impression on a child's mind. It was this capacity for caring for and understanding others that endeared him to people of all ages, and his happiness undoubtedly shines through both his diaries and his drawings.

Thomas Arnold at Brathay

Shortly after the departure of the Hardens in 1830, the famous headmaster of Rugby school, Dr Thomas Arnold, came on the scene. At Rugby he was busy transforming the school into a place where the things that mattered most, much more than learning or athletic prowess, were Christian rectitude, compassion for others, and a willingness to accept responsibility. In 1832, Arnold lodged at the Hall with his considerable family, for a few weeks, while awaiting completion of their own Lake District home, Fox How, a mile or so to the north by the River Rothay. Arnold noted in his diary:

Took possession of Brathay Hall, a large house and large domain. Never was such a renewal of strength and spirits as our children experienced from their six weeks sojourn in this paradise. Our intimacy with the Wordsworths was cemented and scenery and society together made this time a period of enjoyment.

Arnold's sojourn at Brathay was not solely prompted by his new house. A cholera outbreak in Rugby had forced him to end term early and send the boys home. As for his acquaintance with Wordsworth, one wonders how far the poet pushed his idea that 'regular, daily contact with the natural world, with the land and the weather and the changing seasons, has a steadying and ennobling effect on human character'. Or whether Coleridge, among the first to discover the joys of adventurous exploration in the high fells, had an opportunity to push his enthusiasm for the hills:

The farther I ascend from animated Nature, from men, and cattle, and the common birds of the woods and fields, the greater becomes in me the intensity of the feeling of life.

Old Brathay

Old Brathay, too, had a role as an education centre. In 1856 it served as the vicarage. The vicar, the Reverend S.P. Boutflower (a grandson of the Braithwaites who had lived there in 1780 and whose own grandson, the Reverend C.R. Shepherd, was vicar of Brathay from 1939 to 1966), took in as students young men between school and university (what we would now call the 'gap' year). This was a common practice as it enabled clergymen to augment their meagre income. Boutflower must have made quite a business of it since we hear that, to accommodate his students, he added the upper storey to the building.

Giles Redmayne

Some time in the mid-1830s, the Brathay estate was bought by Giles Redmayne, a London draper who had made his money from ribbons. He and his descendants lived there for the next 100 years, and it was he who had Brathay's church built in 1836, with Wordsworth's help in choosing the site. One wonders whether Wordsworth didn't much care for its Romanesque style, as the testimonial he gave it (proudly displayed in the church to this day) sticks strictly to the matter of location: 'There is not a situation outside the Alps or among them more beautiful than this'.

We know of two other famous families who rented the Hall during the Redmaynes' time: the Bells of Yorkshire (Gertrude Bell was the famous writer and traveller) and the Irvings of Liverpool, whose son was lost on Everest with Mallory in 1924.

In 1939, the whole estate was sold to Francis Scott, a successful businessman from Kendal and founder of the Brathay Hall Trust.

THEME 1:
FRANCIS SCOTT'S VISION

Francis Scott was a powerful personality. He had all the confidence of an immensely successful self-made man. He was a workaholic, intelligent, strong-minded and fiercely autocratic. In some ways he was the epitome of the Victorian business magnate: hard-headed in business, cautious but capable of enterprise, and somewhat egocentric. He cared above all else for the family firm, the Provincial Insurance Company. 'Our sole consideration,' he said, 'is profit', the aim is 'superabundant financial strength'. But he also believed that great wealth carried great responsibilities, including that of serving the community through charitable works. In later life, when his fortune was firmly established, he threw himself into charitable activities with all the skill and enthusiasm that he had applied to his business life.

His great achievements were bought at considerable cost to his private life, however. According to his son, Peter Scott, he had a difficult relationship with his family.

He was totally devoted to his work, and he would spend every evening writing letters to people who worked for him, bossing everyone around, wanting to know everything that was going on. He was mad about Brathay! And he loved young people. But he was quite incapable of relaxing. He'd been lamed for life in a bad fall as a child and so he was denied most sports. But he took up yachting and became passionate about it and highly skilled. He won many races on Windermere.

THE PROVINCIAL INSURANCE COMPANY

The Provincial Insurance Company was launched in 1903 in the cotton-spinning town of Bolton. The founder was James Scott, a young man who had done well in the cotton trade and married advantageously. He now used his wife's money – £75,000 – to set up this family business. His eldest son, Samuel, became a director, and Francis, the second son, company secretary. Francis was educated at Bedales, one of the earliest of the progressive boarding schools with an emphasis on the arts and the outdoors, and he later claimed that the school had made a great impact on him. After Bedales he studied at Oriel College, Oxford, and then set about mastering the mysteries and details of the insurance business. By general consensus it was he, more than anyone else, who made the family venture such a resounding success.

He was a keen pioneer motorist and was among the first people to recognise how important car insurance was going to become. His lameness spared him the horrors of military service in the First World War, and he worked on carefully and methodically building up the fortunes of the company. The Lake District had long been a popular holiday place for the Scott family and, in 1919, by which time both sons were married and starting families, the company's headquarters was moved out of the damp smoky atmosphere of Bolton to the cleaner, fresher air of Kendal. Branches were set up all over the UK, and the Provincial soon became the biggest privately-owned insurance firm in the country.

SCOTT BUYS BRATHAY

By 1939, when he purchased the Brathay estate, Francis Scott was managing director of the company and the owner of a handsome house, Matson Ground, just outside Windermere. His first aim for Brathay seems to have been environmental rather than education. He simply wanted the land in order to preserve its natural beauty, to protect it from development, and to use it for either agricultural or recreational purposes. Then he began wondering how he might turn the estate to some more charitable use. Looking back now, there is an almost providential air about how contacts and suggestions came together to lead him towards the Brathay idea.

As a young student at Oxford, Scott had been actively involved in voluntary youth work in London's East End. For many years after that he had devoted himself single-mindedly to the company's affairs, but by the 1930s the pressure was easing and Scott's enquiring mind turned once more to social questions and what might be done about them. He was aware, of course, of the various movements that helped young people – the Boy Scouts, Talbot House (Toc H), and the Boys' Clubs, which he already supported through the sponsorship by Oxford Colleges of clubs in Bermondsey, south London – and then there were the Duke of York's Camps, which brought together boys from industry and public schools. He was also acutely aware of the desperate and widespread unemployment in the industrial areas of West Cumberland.

Dick Faithfull-Davies.

THE NABC INITIATIVES

In 1935 the National Association of Boys' Clubs (NABC) sent a young man to West Cumberland as an Assistant Field Secretary to set up a series of clubs in the region. His name was Dick Faithfull-Davies, but everyone knew him simply as FD. It was Arthur Howard, the local Toc H padre, who introduced FD to Scott, and from this meeting a creative partnership was launched. It was an unpromising partnership in many ways – the tough efficient businessman, and the idealistic inspirational FD – but, for a while at least, they complemented each other most effectively. Scott was impressed by FD's zeal and charm but horrified at the amateur and unbusinesslike way in which he, and the NABC generally, ran its affairs. Scott soon became involved in the foundation of the Cumberland and Westmorland Association of Boys' Clubs and was its first chairman. The local association was generously supported by Scott, but funds also came from the government's West Cumbria Special Areas Fund and from the King George's Jubilee Fund. Scott allowed the Lancashire association to use Brathay for informal weekends, its first use for youth work.

With the outbreak of the Second World War in 1939, the NABC lost many of its leaders to the armed forces and there was a risk of widespread closures. In response to this, the National Youth Service was set up, initially to support the needs of the voluntary groups, but also to expand the service by providing clubs through the local education authorities.

As an additional measure to cope with the manpower shortage, FD inaugurated a scheme called Senior Boy Training to develop older teenagers so that they could take over the running of clubs and camps. The scheme went well, with local courses taking place all over the country. These courses were held over a number of weekends with a progressive programme.

By the early summer of 1940, FD was planning for the boy trainees to come together in a National Gathering. He later wrote:

Our aim was to make the maximum impression within the brief space of a week. With this in mind, our first consideration was not only the picture we intended to paint, but also that it should be set in a frame which would itself be highly memorable. So many of our boys came from drab industrial backgrounds where one week was exactly like another. Our intention was that our week, set in a unique frame, would be recalled in such glowing retrospect that it would have a lasting – even permanent – effect upon impressionable young minds.

Brathay seemed the ideal setting for the gathering and Scott was only too happy to allow it. The National Gathering took place during the week of 8–15 June, 1940, the week France fell to the advancing German tanks. Despite the disaster in Europe, the week was a triumph at Brathay. A total of 79 boys attended. The sun shone. They went fell walking, swimming in the tarns and sailing on the lake. They were taught handicrafts and they produced a play – Lord Dunsany's *The Lord of the Mountains* – which was performed at the end of the week, and a newspaper celebrating their achievements.

Between 1940 and 1945, Brathay Hall was taken over for use as a Church of England Children's Society home for orphan children evacuated from London and the east coast, but the ideals of youth training continued to grow elsewhere.

THE WIDER SCENE

Brian Ware and FD

In 1941, three similar NABC training weeks were held at different locations in England, and this year saw the first arrival of a man who was to play a more enduring and influential role in the Brathay story than anyone else. Brian Ware had grown up in Sussex, but the family holidays were usually taken in the Lake District where he became a keen fell walker. He was interested in youth work and helped in a Toc H boys club in Eastbourne and attended the Duke of York's camps. He studied geography at Cambridge, and then in the autumn of 1940, before joining the Royal Navy for war service, he went to West Cumberland to run the Murray Boys' Club, set in the decaying slums of Whitehaven.

In the course of his duties in the club he came to know well and admire Scott, whose support and wise guidance extended to every aspect of the work. At this time he also met FD in the local Senior Boy Training Courses in Cumberland and Westmorland, and worked with him to organise one of the National Gatherings at the association's Bassenthwaite campsite in 1941. Ware remembers FD as someone of great vision, who was also able to translate his ideas into practical applications.

Brian Ware.

This facility enabled him to attract many first class people into his supporting team. His rapport with young people was remarkable. He spoke very quietly, commanding full attention because he made each group he worked with feel that they were unique and specially capable. There was always a gentle humour behind the serious exterior and this would sometimes erupt in hilarious stories, told in 'pigeon English', of his experiences as a young man in the New Guinea outback. Throughout the war he remained the indefatigable inspiration of the Senior Boy Training concept.

Meanwhile, Ware found that none of the members of the Murray Boys' Club had ever ventured into the nearby fells of the Lake District. Weekend visits to the Bassenthwaite camp changed all that as groups cycled out to cook and look after themselves and to explore the fells. This helped to create a tremendous club spirit.

FD went on running the Senior Boys' Training courses and they proved successful and influential. In *The History of Development Training*, Dr Bertie Everard writes:

The immediate origins of Brathay's distinctive philosophy may be traced directly to the Senior Boy Training initiative of the National Association of Boys' Clubs developed between 1939 and 1945. The courses had an underlying theme of preparing members to play a responsible role in running their clubs. Their distinctive blend of activities had, by the end of the war, been refined into a most effective approach to youth training, and had been adopted by other youth organisations.

In *Brathay – The First 25 Years*, Dr Bruce Campbell lists the War Office, the Admiralty, the National Fire Service, India House, the Royal Empire Society, the Ministry of Information, the BBC and the English Speaking Union as all asking for help in devising similar training schemes for youngsters. The interest of this last organisation led to the running of over 100 boys' and girls' conferences in the USA.

During the war period, other potent influences were at work that were to affect the way people widened the horizons of the younger generation. The Army had taken to using mountain training to enable troops to operate with initiative in small units in harsh conditions. One key training base was the Highland Fieldcraft Training Centre in the Cairngorms, where the commander was at one time Lord Rowallan, later Chief Scout. Included on his staff was Adam Arnold-Brown, who became the first Warden of Outward Bound's first Mountain School in Eskdale in 1950.

The influence of Kurt Hahn

Kurt Hahn was the founder of a progressive school at Castle Salem in Germany in 1920. Unusually for that country it was a boarding school, modelled, Hahn claimed, on Eton; but the approach was entirely his own. The mountaineer and writer Geoffrey Winthrop Young, then an Education Inspector in England and a great friend of Hahn's, comments:

[He was] a practical educator of resource and intuition without his like...combining the more liberal of Plato's educational methods with the better of our public school traditional practices; and he was readjusting the emphasis they placed on brainwork, handiwork, games, the arts and so on. The results were conspicuously successful especially in the higher percentage of boys of average mentality to whom justice was being done.

From the biography *Geoffrey Winthrop Young* by A. Hankinson

In 1933 Hahn fled from Nazi Germany to the UK, and in 1934 he founded Gordonstoun, in the Scottish Highlands, along similar lines to his German school. His desire to help all young people led to the development of an achievement award known as the County Badge. This badge, like the Duke of Edinburgh's Award which succeeded it, emphasised fourfold success in the fields of physical standards, expedition, project and service. One motivation behind the badge for Hahn was his feeling that many young people, because of their urban upbringing and industrial environment, were 'undernourished and soft-boned'. This echoed the sentiments of many in the UK in the mid-1930s, an official response to which had been the Keep Fit Movement. But Hahn wished to go a step further and incorporate the ancient Greek ideal of educating and invigorating the 'whole man'.

The third field in which Hahn was able to apply his ideas was in the founding of Outward Bound. The Outward Bound Sea School at Aberdovey came into being in 1941 with the very practical aim of preserving lives at sea. Many Merchant seamen were being lost because, it was felt,

Map of Brathay from the first brochure, Holidays with Purpose.

THE BRATHAY HALL CENTRE

they lacked the resourcefulness to cope with the crisis of a sinking ship. Thanks to the generosity of Laurence Holt, the owner of a shipping line, who provided the house, a training ship and most of the staff, Hahn was able to put into practice an amalgam of his ideas from both Gordonstoun and the Badge Scheme. The result was the challenge–and activity-based courses that have since become so well known. Hahn's attitude towards adventure and challenge is perhaps summed up in his famous comment:

No boy should be compelled into opinions, but it is criminal negligence not to impel him into experience.
                                                                                          Letter to *The Times*, 5 April, 1938.

THE WAR AND AFTER

The desire to do something better for young people can be traced back to the end of the First World War and the 'Fisher' Education Act, 1918. This made the school-leaving age 14 years, but stated that until the age of 18 years, everyone must remain in touch with the national education system through one day a week day-release from their jobs to what were called Day Continuation Schools.

Although this idea failed to get off the ground because of the many financial crises during the interwar period, the idea lingered and re-emerged in the Education Act, 1944. As A.E. Morgan says in his book *Young Citizen* (Penguin, 1943), wars have a habit of making people look to the future:

One of the most potent spurs to action is fear, and that is why war may lead to reforms which in the complacent mood of peace we are unwilling to effect. War makes a peculiar threat to the race of tomorrow, and in our fear we may think more carefully of the youth on whom tomorrow depends. It is not that it creates a youth problem, although it may produce certain unusual features. The youth problem is eternal. It is the problem which education ever attempts to solve.

The Education Act, 1944, proposed the setting up of County Colleges, which everyone would attend either for one day a week, or for a four-week residential period once a year. The colleges were not primarily for vocational training but for an all-round liberal education; a chance for young people to follow their interests, to widen their horizons, to learn more of the world and their responsibilities therein. Sport, adventure and outdoor activities were to be a key part of the programmes.

Scott was a member of the Westmorland Education Committee and must have been well aware of the discussions leading up to the 1944 act. He may have seen Brathay as a prototype County College as the original Trust deed seems to envisage this. But with memories fresh of what did not happen after the First World War, Scott must have concluded that it would be wiser to 'go it alone'. In the event, he clearly made the right decision as the County College scheme foundered, but it is interesting to note that in the subsequent national debate Brathay was thought of as a prototype County College.

The Crowther report

The Crowther report was the result of an examination of the education of all young people between the ages of 15 and 18 years. It was published in 1959 and included the following paragraph.

Since 1944, important advances have been made with educational schemes which have developed quite outside the county college concept, but which will have to be integrated with it. The experience of the Outward Bound and Brathay Hall experiments, and with the Duke of Edinburgh's Award, for instance, have shown that there are forms of training, in which physical challenge and response play a large part, which have made a strong appeal to many young people. Their contribution ought to be recognised and made use of in any national system.

Reproduced with the permission of the Controller of HMSO

The report said that although there had been a great expansion in day release after the Second World War, this had been 'very largely for boys and almost entirely for training for skilled craftsmen or technicians. No real impression has been made on the young unskilled workers or on girls in employment'.

SETTING UP THE BRATHAY TRUST

The NABC Senior Boy Training courses came to an end with the return of the servicemen after the war. But what FD had created in those courses was too good to lose, and shortly afterwards, together with Scott, he obtained a brief to put together a new course, to be open to all and to be run by a new, totally independent foundation. This was the beginning of Brathay as it is today.

In his 'Statement of Intent' written many years later, Scott acknowledges his debt to Outward Bound:

Our acquisition of the Brathay estate, originally for preservation purposes in the public interest, led almost inevitably to the problem of what use to make of the amenities offered, and it was in the eventual decision to make our own experiment in a modification of the 'Outward Bound' concept to which the formation of the Brathay Hall Trust owes its origin.

Nevertheless, it is soon apparent that much of the thinking behind the course is quite different (in fact, John Doogan, a later warden, often used to say that the only thing Brathay had in common with Outward Bound was the length of the course!), and the Brathay centre began some four years before the Outward Bound Mountain School. Indeed, Brathay was probably the first ever mountain training centre for youths from industry.

The Trust deed

Scott's aim was the 'opening [of] young people's minds to the possibilities of living adventurously in the world of physical activity as well as in the world of the spirit'.

The objectives of the new centre, as stated in the Trust deed, were:

- The establishment and maintenance of a centre or centres in any part of Great Britain for the education, including the physical training and moral, intellectual and physical development of young persons of both sexes from industry within the United Kingdom.
- The initiation and prosecution – whether at the said centres or elsewhere – of investigation and research into questions affecting the education of such persons.
- The instruction of the staff of such centres and other persons to qualify them to promote the purposes aforesaid.
- Any other charitable purposes of an educational nature which can be promoted in combination with all or any of the purposes aforesaid.

This deed opened the door for all the many and varied activities that were to be the life of Brathay in the years ahead. The second and third clauses point prophetically to aspects of Brathay's work that were to make it so influential in the world of development training: its role as the philosopher of the new education, constantly experimenting with fresh ideas and techniques, and its role as a training school for the trainers themselves.

In *The History of Development Training*, Everard comments:

This [deed] is unique among Development Training providers and has been responsible for Brathay being an innovator at the leading edge of Development Training. Despite the fact that 'Outward Bound' is better known to the general public, Brathay has been generally recognised as the mother house of the Development Training profession and the pedagogical leader of the pack.

FD, in one of his campaigning documents, described the aims of the Brathay Trust in less legal language:

...an awakening of some potentiality or hidden gift in the child; an understanding or a beginning of an appreciation of communal life; a realisation of the individual's importance in the making of a community; the beginning of a sense of personal significance and with it the first step towards self-confidence; the wish for bodily fitness; a desire for beauty in life and surroundings and so perhaps the start of a healthy resentment of ugliness and squalor.

And Scott himself underlined and added to those sentiments:

There should be a minimum of rules to be observed but a clear understanding that privileges equally demand acceptance of certain restraints voluntarily accepted and it should be the aim to prove to those attending courses that nothing worthwhile is achieved which does not demand some measure of self-discipline and self-denial.

BRATHAY BEGINS

Now came the task of putting all these statements into practice and forming a working body. The meeting of the Brathay Hall trustees that took place on 30 July, 1946 is generally regarded as the

start of the new Brathay. It was presided over by Scott and attended by his son Peter, by S.G. Lewis, headmaster of Windermere Grammar School, R.L. Hall, who owned the Langdale estates cultural and holiday centre and took a keen interest in youth work, and FD, who had already been made warden. They appointed O. Gillespie of Martins Bank, Ambleside, as treasurer.

FD set about preparing the first courses. The aim was to provide a multi-activity week based on the earlier experiences of the NABC training courses, although this time the purpose was not leader training but a general broadening of the experience of life. Most youngsters then left school at 14, and, as Brian Ware had found in Whitehaven, their experience of the outdoors was often very limited. For many, school had offered little in the way of art, drama, or even physical education, and the chance of a holiday had been a remote prospect. But the post-war period brought two new benefits: a reduction in the working week to five days, compared with five and a half or six days previously, and a much wider implementation of holidays with pay.

Holidays with Purpose

Perhaps as an echo of this last innovation, the courses were called Holidays with Purpose, and were aimed at 14- and 15-year-old industrial apprentices. Scott approached his vast range of contacts among businessmen in the north of England for help. Prominent among the industrial supporters was Graham Satow, a director of the Corby steel firm Stewarts and Lloyds, who had a home in Langdale. He was an influential person in the world of industrial training and one-time chairman of the British Association for Commercial and Industrial Education (BACIE).

The Hall was fitted out with 24 beds for the boys in the dormitories on the first and second floors, plus rooms for six members of staff. Post-war shortages prevented a fuller use of the facilities. Staff were recruited, establishing the Brathay tradition of a high student: trainer ratio, and posters and leaflets were produced.

Among the visiting staff was an inspirational artist called Walter Spradbery. He had been art adviser to the NABC and worked on the Senior Boy Training courses. FD had been much impressed by his enthusiasm and had noted the popularity of his teaching methods. It was Spradbery's strong influence that created Brathay's reputation for original and highly effective work in art and handicrafts, and he always took great inspiration from his fellow east Anglian, Constable, who had lived and painted at Brathay over a century before.

Brian Ware, just back from the Far East and demobilised from the Navy, went to see his parents, who then lived at Coniston. They told him that FD was up to something at Brathay, and so Ware hurried over to find out what was going on. FD asked him to help, and Ware joined the team as Number Two in March 1947.

The brochure

The courses were soon established and the 1949 brochure gives a very good picture of the aims and activities on these courses.

The programmes vary from week to week and are influenced by the different enthusiasms of

BRATHAY

1953

Holidays for Boys

the boys and the particular qualifications of the voluntary staff. Within the limitations of growing boys, who are seldom as fit as we would wish to see them, our outdoor activities are fairly strenuous, but, since we see no point in sending them back to work exhausted, we do not make a fetish out of 'toughness'.

Our basic outdoor pursuits are sailing, rowing, swimming, mountaineering, bird-watching, sketching and various kinds of games. Indoors, the Brathay Little Theatre gives weekly shows which are well supported by local residents. Here boys learn something both of teamwork and self-expression and reap an immediate reward of effort in the appreciation shown by their audiences. The preparation and publishing of the Brathay News *is another weekly event which teaches valuable lessons and provides tangible results, and our Art studios, having shown their worth by a steady output of drawings, paintings and lino-cuts, have been enlarged and greatly improved. Other indoor activities, no less useful though the results may not be immediately apparent, are talks, readings, discussions, film shows and musical recitals. Our games room has been reconstructed to provide first rate conditions for table tennis. The usual quiet games such as chess and draughts are played in the library.*

It may seem odd to include household duties in the list of valuable indoor activities, but we find that men and boys working together at tasks such as the cleaning of their rooms, preparation of vegetables and washing up does much to produce a willing spirit and good morale.

Later in the brochure's kit list, we find: 'Each boy is given a free issue of nailed boots, shirt, shorts, thick socks, sweater, battle-blouse, rubber cape, towel and rucksack.'

A staff reminiscence

A member of the training staff, Stanley Cain, recalled those pioneering days thus:

Brathay was to reach out to the boys of the post-war generation by utilising the new phenomenon of holidays with pay and offering them something different, wider, more imaginative; something they would remember all their days. Since each course only lasted one week, our abiding principle was to make the maximum impression in the minimum time. The programme had three 'musts': to climb Helvellyn or Scafell, to produce the Brathay News, *and to stage a one and a half hour show in the Little Theatre. This*

Setting out to survey a mountain tarn.

'theatre' was a room in the Hall [now the bar] fitted with a temporary stage and with exits and entrances for the actors through the windows. We were fortunate with the voluntary staff we collected – artists, bird-watchers, musicians, sailors, mountaineers, and doctors. Though some activities were minority pursuits, they blended in most satisfactorily with the more strenuous ones which attracted the majority. We made something of a feature of high-altitude camping, when boys stayed on the tops for a night or more. Sometimes we had a regatta of sorts or a swimming gala in the lake.

One activity that became a regular part of the courses was going into the hills and mapping the outlines and depths of the high mountain tarns. Out of this work grew the Brathay Exploration Group (described in Theme 3).

The apprentices who came to Brathay were greatly handicapped when it came to fell walking since many of them, because of their backgrounds, were in a poor physical condition. Cain recalls:

Early in the afternoon of Day One the boys and volunteers arrived and we carried out our normal routine – issue of kit, sorting into dormitories and a medical once-over by the volunteer doctor, who then passed them to FD. As an ardent believer in happy feet, he scrubbed every foot, trimmed toenails, cut out ingrowing ones, treated tinea pedis [athlete's foot] and such complaints, squatting on a wooden stool by the surgery footbath and talking to every boy individually.

The course cost £3.10s. a week, and it was suggeested that if a boy could not afford the full amount, his firm should help him out with, say, £1. The brochure said that a modest subsidy was preferable to a large one since that way a firm could be persuaded to help more boys to attend.

The convalescence scheme

Despite their success, holiday courses alone could not justify the development of Brathay as a centre for young people. There was a suggestion that it might be offered as a conference centre, but FD thought the place was probably too basic for that. Nevertheless, it was advertised and there was some use as such, although no records remain except for an observation that the steel firm Richard Thomas and Baldwins came and was so keen on it that it wanted to buy the place!

The principal back-up use was as a place where boys from industrial backgrounds who were recovering from serious illnesses might come for a week or two for recuperation.

Scott called it 'an experiment in healing'. He said that the activities of the holiday courses could be adapted and applied 'in aid of convalescence and rehabilitation' for those who were on the way to recovery 'but who yet required to regain a fuller measure of health and confidence in their powers of recovery, mental and physical, before they return to work'.

Cain remembers two of the many boys who came to Brathay under this scheme:

There was a boy with a bronchial system 'shot to bits' who came for two visits. He ended up being able to play a vigorous game of shinty and then left to join the Navy. Charlie, from Dumfries, aged 15, had been in hospital since the age of eight with incurable heart disease. He was given as much as possible of the things he had missed in life. They even carried him to the top of Todd Crag to be photographed to send to his doctor saying 'this is me, 1000ft up'. He produced a play, edited Brathay News, *fashioned puppets, painted, sketched, and even sailed. He planted a garden and eventually was able to present a bouquet to Betty Faithfull-Davies. This symbolised his example and influence and finally crystallised our feeling that the Brathay spirit must be something that far transcended mere cliff-hanging.*

One of the recurring themes of Brathay's history is the tension that arises between two contrasting types of people. On the one hand there are the high-minded enthusiasts, in Brathay's case mostly young men, who were happy to work very hard indeed for little pay, for the privilege of helping adolescent boys from industrial backgrounds to broaden their horizons and develop new skills, interests and self-confidence. On the other hand, there are the business-minded realists who know that, however noble and enlightened the cause, someone has to think about money and marketing, keep the accounts and look ahead. The tension can be creative and stimulating, serving to keep both types on their toes.

FD was no businessman. He did not concern himself with money. His overriding interest was in providing the best possible service for the boys. The necessary money, he felt sure, could always be found later. Neither was he an administrator, much preferring to be where the training was to sitting in the office. Scott, on the other hand, was a dedicated businessman. He believed in the virtue of proper professional business procedures and in keeping a close eye on what was going on at Brathay. Inevitably, there were misunderstandings and disagreements, and it was as a result of one of these that FD's tenure as the first warden came to an end with his premature departure in September 1949.

After three years of Holidays with Purpose and Winter Convalescent Breaks, it became clear that these alone, however worthy, did not make for a fully active and financially viable centre. Something more permanent and long-term was needed. A new chapter in the life of Brathay was about to begin.

THEME 2:
THE FOUR-WEEK COURSES

All the experience of the previous schemes was now about to bear fruit in the establishment of a standard course that would meet the needs and aspirations of the time so successfully. The course that so many people were to remember all their lives was about to be born.

Although government had expressed hopes of setting up residential centres, Francis Scott was not a man to wait for guidance from the government. Graham Satow and Scott's other advisers, including people from the steel firm Richard Thomas & Baldwins who had supported Holidays with Purpose, persuaded Scott that what industry wanted was a *four-week course* based on the successful pattern of activities already developed.

Dr Bertie Everard has written thus about what industry expected of these courses:

The assumption that underlay the Brathay experience was that all young people had hidden potential which could be unlocked by the experience, with flowering of inner strength, self-respect, natural pride, self-discipline and a sense of responsibility. Without the opportunity to display such qualities, adolescents sometimes assumed an attitude, varying from one individual to another, but showing up in such ways as aggressiveness, cocksureness, indifference or insecurity. The course enabled boys to discover their real capabilities, to experience the satisfaction of community, teamwork and creativity, and to be encouraged to try out new pursuits for enjoyment rather than for endurance.

JOHNNY MACMILLAN

Johnny Macmillan was to be the dominant force at Brathay for the next three years. Brian Ware, who saw much of him from his own post as honorary secretary of the fast-growing Brathay Exploration Group (see Theme 3), described him as 'an extraordinary man, very dynamic, very left wing, a mixture of high religious and political fervour'. This was the period when the 'Cold War' between the Communist eastern bloc and the capitalist West was beginning to intensify. Scott, strong in his Christian faith and among the most successful of capitalists, must have harboured doubts about a man as politically different from him as Macmillan was. But it was in Macmillan's favour that he, too, was a dedicated Christian, a leading disciple of the charismatic George Macleod, founder of the Iona Community in Scotland, which had a very active mission in the shipyards of Glasgow. Macmillan had run the popular youth camps on Iona, combining outdoor holidays with rebuilding the old abbey there as a retreat house for the community.

Macmillan arrived at Brathay in April 1950 and appointed two men who were to exert great influence over Brathay's progress: Douglas Hayward, who became a key figure in the Exploration Group and in the Duke of Edinburgh's Award when that was set up in 1956, and George Pettingale. Later, when Pettingale went on to become principal of a 'special school' in Oxfordshire, he brought parties of maladjusted boys from there to camp at Brathay each year. These camps were to mark the start of the tradition of using Brathay to help young people with personality problems.

THE BROCHURE

The small brochure produced to advertise the new courses contained the following preamble:

As a result of experience gained during the past four years, and after consultation with a number of representatives of industry, the Trustees have decided that the Centre shall, from the end of summer 1950, direct its energies towards the provision of One-Month Residential Courses for boys in industry. We are anxious to serve boys in Industry in the widest sense which may enrich their own lives and may enable them to serve best their day and generation.

The centre will be run on the lines of a community. Thus not only will many boys learn for the first time what it means to have to stand on their own feet. They will also, as members of a community, make their contribution to the domestic and social routine...The emphasis of the Centre is that of the Christian life, and voluntary attendance at morning and evening prayers is part of each day's activity.

The permanent teaching staff...will be in the ratio of one leader to 10 or 12 boys. Except that they have their own bedrooms, the leaders share fully in the life of the community at Brathay. The atmosphere of friendliness and co-operation combined with the demands of discipline – essential in any ordered life – enable the boy to feel that he is experiencing a grown-up relationship with the Staff.

In view of the current practice of agreeing on ground rules and contracts through discussion at the start of a course, it is interesting to find this observation (and aspiration) from almost 50 years ago:

A system of full self-government will not be practicable in the limited time at the disposal of the Centre, but the boys will be encouraged to run, or assist in running, as many as possible of the various undertakings of the Centre.

COURSE AIMS

The aims of the courses were defined as:

● *to promote development of character through self-reliance, self-discipline, resourcefulness, tenacity of purpose, and a creative attitude of mind*
● *to create an increased awareness of the responsibilities of the individual to society*
● *to broaden outlook and increase mental zest*
● *to encourage the enjoyment of physical activity.*

Working time is spent on the mountains and lake, in the workshop, and undertaking various other activities. In following an intensive programme they may well be required to face adverse weather in difficult country, which can contribute much to the development of real hardiness. Instruction in all activities is comprehensive. Map-reading, compasses, meteorology, camp-craft, etc. in mountain work lead to expeditions of several days' duration. On the water there is a range of tuition designed to ensure some competence not only in sailing but also in general boatwork. On the Estate, in the workshop and in the Craft studio, there is an opportunity for learning, an application of that learning to purposeful tasks...At the conclusion of each course a full report on each boy is sent to his employers. Records and reports of Courses will, in due course, provide a valuable basis for investigation in the field of boy training.

THE MEMORIES OF ONE COURSE MEMBER

Perhaps the best description of those early days comes from the memories of a former course member. By a happy coincidence, while this book was being written, one of the apprentices who attended a course in 1951 turned up at Brathay. His wife, knowing how much that long ago course had meant to him, had arranged a return visit as a holiday surprise for his 60th birthday. His name is John Foster, and he was moved by his return, which brought back many vivid memories.

I attended Brathay in September 1951 just before my 16th birthday. I was a typical youth of that time. I had never been away from home apart from one holiday on a farm during the war, and I had not shined well at grammar school. I was an engineering apprentice, not through choice but because my father wanted me to have a trade. My first sight of Brathay, Wansfell, and Windermere stays in my mind for ever. I naively thought that because I enjoyed football, athletics, boxing and swimming I would excel at the tasks outlined to us by the team leaders. In fact I found the four weeks the most difficult I have ever endured. Did we really swim in the lake at daybreak, walk from early morning to late afternoon, sail a large ketch from the inlet down the length of Windermere and walk back fully-laden, work in the forest with the woodsmen, be on the fells for three days in torrential rain! Every one of us at some time in the month felt like just sitting down and giving in. Facing what seemed like insurmountable problems and having to make decisions that would affect the group was very daunting to a 15-year-old.

I was lucky to be able to return to Brathay in 1952 and 1953 at my own expense for two weeks each time (with the Exploration Group) helping to carry out research work on projects such as lake depths, wind speeds and directions...

It was only on reflection that I understood and appreciated what Brathay had meant to me in my youth and what it has been to me throughout my life. I was proud of what I had achieved. I had more self-esteem and confidence to face the future. Almost 30 years later I met one of my old Apprentice Training Officers. He had originally selected me to go to Brathay firstly because of my efforts in the first year, but more importantly because he felt I needed it to help my confidence and self-awareness. He had no doubts at all that my employment achievements, personal development, and outlook on life had been initiated at Brathay...Brathay introduced me to another world.

Foster's working life was in engineering until 1983 when he went to staff a government Youth Training Scheme.

Brathay even helped my appreciation for this work, because we were setting up a residential course for youngsters in mid-Wales. Many of the kids came from underprivileged families and had special needs and behavioural problems, some had probationary records. It was very rewarding to utilise my experience to introduce and develop an awareness in them of their potential. Inner-city life tends to produce bullies. [But in the hills we found] an amazing pattern that repeated itself: that the introverts and those who had been bullied often outshone the 'tough' guys and girls.

Foster concluded by reflecting again on his return visit to Brathay.

There are many alterations to the outer buildings, dormitories and the boat house, but I was thrilled to find the spirit, aims and feel of the place exactly as I remembered it. Long may it continue to inspire future generations of young men and women.

Former Brathay trainees like Foster frequently call in to say hello and to refresh their memories of the place. Like Foster, they are invariably moved to voice heart-felt and quite unsolicited testimonials about what the Brathay experience had done for them.

PERSONALITIES

There are few records remaining from the Macmillan era, but it seems that much time had to be devoted to enlisting the support of firms for the new courses. A strong ally was Sir Ronald Nesbitt-Hawes, chief of education administration with the English Electric Co. Ltd. The Venerable Mervyn Armstrong, a future Bishop of Jarrow, also had useful industrial connections. On the resident staff was Clare Charteris who, like Macmillan, came from the Iona Community. Officially in place as secretary, Charteris was able to turn her hand to almost anything – an essential virtue in any small but growing establishment – from stoking boilers to reading prayers, seeing to Lights Out, and country dancing.

Two men who were to be involved for a long time arrived in 1952: Alan Barrett, from the Scottish Council for Physical Recreation Centre at Glenmore Lodge, who came as sailing instructor but was to end up as administrative head, and John Doogan. Doogan was initially appointed as bursar, but was ultimately to become warden and the presiding spirit for almost a decade.

Macmillan left in 1953 to join the full-time staff of Toc H, and his place was taken by John Thompson, a master from Clifton College. However, Thompson left at the end of 1954 to take up the headship of Keswick School, and so, at the turn of the year, Doogan took over as warden. Tragically, his promotion coincided with the death of his wife, Pat, who had played a very full part in making Brathay a home from home for so many people.

Management of Brathay was now largely devolved by the trustees to a Management Committee. This was formed in 1953 and, besides Scott, included Satow as chairman, Nesbitt-Hawes, Armstrong, and John Marsh. Marsh was director of the Industrial Welfare Society (later the Industrial Society), and this link was to prove invaluable for a number of reasons in later years. One other person who became involved during this period was John Trevelyan. He was director of education for Westmorland and had been closely involved in the early days of the Brathay Exploration Group as its first Chairman of Council. Later, he became known to every film-goer in that era as the secretary of the British Board of Film Censors.

In 1957, the committee gained great strength from the inclusion of Hamish (later to be Sir James) Blair-Cunynghame, a prominent member of the National Coal Board (and a colleague of Kurt 'small-is-beautiful' Schumacher), and later to become chairman of the Royal Bank of Scotland. There was also Niall Macdiarmid, chairman of the steel firm Stewarts & Lloyds.

John Doogan and the Brathay courses

Without doubt John Doogan was the dominant character of the next few years and the one people remember so well. Ware recalls Doogan with admiration:

All Brathay's interests came together in him. He had a good sound business background, having run a big department store in Stirling. He had been a soldier in the war, ending up as a Major in the 'forgotten army' in Burma. He had a wonderful sense of humour and could get along fine with young people. He was a musician and an artist and a keen mountain man as well.

The following view of life under Doogan is taken from *Brathay – The First 25 Years* by Dr Bruce Campbell.

The phase which the Brathay experiment entered with the appointment of John Doogan as Warden has been regarded as a sort of golden age. He…was a man of mature years, a friendly 'father figure' to the hundreds of boys with whom he was to come into contact, and he had great gifts in establishing right relationships both with adults and young people. His creed…was 'human understanding is the greatest need and no technique can ever supply it'. He also had the advantage of a singularly talented and devoted staff: in addition to Alan Barrett, David Price, one of the main architects of the four-week courses…came in 1954, and Maurice Dybeck, in 1955, the first chief instructor. A geographer by training he had been a leader on the first Brathay Iceland expedition in 1953 and his particular interest in film-making has

*John Doogan
with Rags.*

been of great service in publicising Brathay's aims and achievements. All three refer to the spontaneity and humour which enlivened so much that John Doogan did in those first years. At a conference in London, Alan Barrett described him as 'warden, chairman and washer-up', and recalls how they competed to put a face and a Christian name to all members of a course in 24 hours. Courses would unexpectedly break routine, perhaps with a race up Todd Crag after the final concert. Doogan...believed boys should be allowed to commit their own mistakes. Dybeck remembers making a huge detour on one expedition until the boy leader discovered his navigational error and corrected it.

As for the deeper values behind a course, a representative of one of the largest industrial federations reported: 'Religion is practised, not preached. One attendance at daily prayers before turning in would be quite enough to convince anyone that the value of worship has become apparent to all and, to many, for the first time in their lives.'

On a lighter note, we find that the same report includes the following:

The trainees do all the household chores other than cooking and, once again, team spirit quells any resentment on the part of those who have never in their lives lent a hand with such things and have left them entirely to an overworked mother...The Warden has had many grateful letters from parents making particular mention of the help they have received in the house since their sons took a course at Brathay Hall and there is little doubt that other lessons learnt such as thinking of others and lending them a hand must have a profound and lasting effect.

Breakfast on the summit of Scafell Pike.

Alan Evans looks back

Alan Evans had the unique experience of coming on a course as a boy and, many years later, becoming an instructor. He remembers it thus:

I grew up as a working class boy, had the basic state education and left school at 15 with no knowledge at all of the arts: the pleasures of reading, art, classical music. I got a job as an apprentice with an enlightened American firm called the Carborundum Company. I showed some talent for engineering drawing and, in 1955, won the Best Apprentice Award. The prize was a month at Brathay. I'd never heard of the place but I went and immediately fell in love with it. John Doogan astonished me. He welcomed us all and said:

'It does rain here but don't worry about that. It'll be great. The bad weather days are the ones you remember.' And it did rain. And it was great!

The thing that most impressed Evans was not the mountaineering – he had already done that – but the cultural revelations.

I was gob-smacked by the classical music. It was absolutely fantastic! The tutors were brilliant: in drama, communication, sketching and painting the outdoor activities, everything. And the other great thing was the Exploration Group. I joined them and went on several expeditions and a whole new world was opened up.

Some reminiscences from Doogan's first chief instructor

1. John Doogan did not have any understanding of the need for days off. His life was his work and others were expected to think likewise. And we all did.

2. Some of my most memorable moments were the high level camps. On two successive courses I arranged that we should colonise the summit of Scafell Pike. And, as a community service, we rebuilt the large memorial viewing platform there. Evening prayers, gathered there above the cloud-filled valleys, was unforgettable.

3. A duty day began well before seeing the boys out of bed. Thanks to Alan Barrett's enthusiasm, the Hall was a thrice-daily weather reporting station for the Met. Office, so Duty Bloggs had to be out at 0645h observing and encoding the weather before ringing it through to Preston.

4. We got into some pretty ambitious play productions. *Macbeth*, in which, for the banquet, John turned out all his best silver, and I hope he got it all back. For *Romeo and Juliet*, our over enthusiastic course electrician 'fixed' the lights so that, at full load, we blew the 'company's fuse' with the result that the show went on by candle-light. And most effective it was too.

5. We were still in post-war shortages and ex-Army gear was often the norm; commando rucksacks, gas cape waterproofs, bivvy tents and square billy cans. But nevertheless good stuff, though heavy. First aid kits I made up using the cook's bulk Oxo cube tins. And, when the maps crumpled in the wet, I discovered a transparent food bag material called Porosan – this was before the days of polybags.

6. Boys were encouraged to bring musical instruments. For those who played the piano there was the chance of using a good grand in the Music Room. But for others there was the old upright in the next room, open for anyone to use, another 'voyage of discovery' for some (but you had to put up with 'chopsticks' rather often!).

7. Perhaps for all instructors the most anxious moments on any course were when you were waiting towards the end of their first day out alone on the final exercise: the Three Day Expedition. They had to ring in and say they were OK. They always were. And the best moment was when they returned, tired but happy, no longer a rag-bag of individuals but a team.

8. And that week of calm between the courses? In fact two whole days were usually filled with an extended staff meeting at which we all prepared those reports on the boys.

THE NATIONAL BACKGROUND

The social scene

It is easy to think that social conditions improved quickly after the Second World War, but as the following extract from the Newsom report of 1963 shows, many people continued to live in virtual slum conditions.

The children live in back-to-back houses which are badly designed, badly lit, and have no indoor sanitation. Few of the children living here have ever seen a bathroom, and in some houses there is not even a towel and soap. Canals and railway lines run alongside the houses giving bad smells, grime and smoke and noise. All these homes have overcrowded living and sleeping quarters. For example, 10 or 11 people may sleep in two beds and one cot. The living room usually measures about 10ft x 9ft and combines gas stove, cupboard, sink and small table. The children are restricted to playing in the small yard or pavement of the main road.

The educational background of many in the earliest post-war years was scarcely more promising. Taught in old, poorly equipped schools in class sizes of well over 30, 40 or more, very few stayed on beyond the school leaving age, which was 14 until 1947 and 15 until 1972.

While a tremendous amount of energy went into building new schools, with the construction of some 1800 new secondary schools between 1954 and 1961, the hopes of improving the opportunities for young people after school were short-lived. The aspirations of the 1944 Education Act and its day release scheme (see Theme 1) largely came to nought, and although there was an increasing awareness among industrialists of the ideals of the early philanthropists such as the Cadburys, and the concept that employers' responsibilities went beyond simply paying wages, very little actually changed for the majority of young working people.

The Albemarle report

Concerns about the lack of provision of opportunities for young people led the government to commission the Albemarle committee to 'review the contribution the Youth Service...can make in assisting young people to play their part in the life of the community, in the light of changing industrial and social conditions'.

The Albemarle report, published in 1960, was critical of the state the Youth Service had been allowed to fall into. It said: '[it] has not been given the treatment it hoped for and has suffered in morale and public esteem in consequence'. There was praise, however, for the work of organisations such as Brathay, and it is clear from the report that Brathay influenced the thoughts behind the committee's findings, as the following extract shows:

The opportunities for challenge which crop up in the life of the group have a special value for the non-academic boy or girl. Physical adventure has the most obvious appeal. To many of the young their world is a humdrum affair; their lives are tram-lined by the streets and time-tabled by the running of buses and trains. The colourful and the unexpected do not happen to them...unless they make it. They can do so by violence, destructiveness or deliberate breaches of accepted public behaviour. Or they can go out of the towns to find it. Scouting and Guiding and kindred movements and, more recently, Outward Bound and Brathay have shown the young a variety of approaches to the object of their search. Some of these schemes have helped the young to find the colourful and unexpected constructively, even in an urban environment and in the workaday setting of home and work. Others [and this must be a reference to the Brathay Exploration Group] *have taken them to a strange environment and shown them how, through strenuous physical effort, they can find powers in themselves they had not known.*

On the value of the residential experience, the report says:

To be a member of a group, living side by side for a period in camp or on an expedition, can be of special value to social development. Experience of the same kind can be gained from residential courses, which many witnesses have praised for the greater impact they make on young people and the opportunities they give for more stimulating and far-reaching work. Their value is all the greater if they also give young people a chance of attending a series of progressively more exacting courses over a period of years.

The Albemarle report led to a great national improvement in youth provision including a leader training centre at Leicester. While this brought no financial help to Brathay, it all indicated that Brathay was in the mainstream of thinking and must have influenced many in deciding to send people on courses or to emulate elsewhere what Brathay was doing.

National Service

As part of our defence in the 'Cold War', two years of National Service remained obligatory for all young men until 1958, and this had the effect of slicing right through any possible progression in career from youth to maturity. *Citizens of Tomorrow*, a report produced in 1955 by the King

George's Jubilee Trust, spoke repeatedly about the uncertainty that was bred into the young worker by the period of 15 to 18 years of age. He saw no point in settling to a regular job because National Service loomed, and employers were reluctant to take on people who would shortly disappear into the forces.

On the positive side, it must be said that many people found their National Service a beneficial experience, widening their horizons, giving them an experience of community living, and training them – perhaps for the first time since they left school – in a wide variety of skills. The aims of an army are, necessarily, fundamentally different from the aims of a factory or a local community, but when conscription was abolished there was a feeling that some of its methods ought to be preserved in the field of youth work. The Albemarle report put it thus:

Many gained immensely from these radically altered ways of life. With the ending of National Service, the Youth Service ought to try and replace some at least of these lost opportunities, and this makes the case for residential and venture courses all the stronger.

We have referred to the value of residential courses, and several authorities have shown how a centre can be used efficiently to provide opportunities both for leadership courses and for weekend or longer visits by groups of young people. We recommend that the expansion of residential provision should have immediate attention in development schemes.

Waiting, with a wealth of experience gained since 1946, Brathay was to be the venue for the first of the leadership courses, which owed much to the approaches pioneered in the Army.

The responsibilities of industry

The statutory provision for industry to provide training for young people dates back to 1563. A Statute of Artifices of that year remained in force for 400 years. Its successor came in 1964 with the establishment of the Industry Training Boards. But whatever the legal requirements, there was a feeling that it was a moral duty of employers to look after their people. The 1955 report *Citizens of Tomorrow* put it thus:

To an ever-increasing extent employers are operating welfare schemes which provide not only for the health and safety of their young employees but also for their recreation and continued education...[We] suggest that more and more employers should be persuaded to follow this example and to regard the 15- to 18-year-old boy or girl as in trust to them, and that they should combine in a special effort to encourage and to facilitate the further education of all their young employees.

We compared these responsibilities of the modern employer to those of the Master towards his charge under the medieval system of apprenticeship, and which, very significantly, included responsibility for the apprentice's religious education and spiritual welfare.

One of the Working Party that wrote *Citizens of Tomorrow* was Satow, who at that time (1954) was also chairman of Outward Bound, Eskdale, as well as chairman of the Brathay Management Committee.

THE STEADY GROWTH OF THE FOUR-WEEK COURSES

In 1958, the number of 'delegate days' attributable to the four-week courses probably just passed 10,000 (a delegate day is defined as one day attended by one delegate/trainee/student). There were nine courses a year, and the accommodation stood at 47 beds. It is interesting to note how that course size was arrived at. To Scott, the magic number in a group was nine: an odd number that prevented an even and possibly disruptive split, but a large enough group to be resourceful and economic to handle. This worked well in the five main dormitory rooms that defined the work group. Soon, however, Windermere and Ullswater, the larger first floor rooms, each became 10-bedded, probably to cope with demand. However, Scott was firmly against courses becoming much bigger, such as those at Outward Bound, where the basic group size was 12 with courses of 72 or more.

Over the years the accommodation and facilities steadily improved (see Appendix A). A staff common room cabin was donated by Satow in 1954, and the big boathouse and launching ramp were built in 1955, at which time each dormitory was equipped with a Wayfarer sailing dinghy and a whaler for rowing. Some of these whalers survive in full use to this day. In 1956, as a joint facility for the Hall and Old Brathay, a 16-bed dormitory block was built on the foundations of an old greenhouse.

In 1958, a new brochure was published and it sums up well what Brathay was seeking to do in these now well-established courses (although the founder's aim of helping 'young persons of both sexes' seems to have been ignored).

The greatest need, in the immensely complex world of today, is not for new machines but for new men. For whole men, for balanced men, for men of good report...The courses at Brathay Hall are designed to provide a natural opportunity, in a communal setting, for a boy to discover for himself the many latent qualities he has within him.

We are not a school, let alone a forcing house, for heroes. Our approach is creative. The activities of the Brathay course – boatwork and mountain craft, discussion, art and acting – all have equal parts to play towards enabling the individual to experience within himself the status of a whole man. A man that is unafraid of giving a good account of himself; a man with his self-respect intact. To enjoy, to encourage and to entrust is the Brathay way. Here he learns that responsibility in a community is the most satisfying and self-respecting form of discipline. He discovers that true leadership is not a matter so much of giving orders as of responsibly understanding people and situations.

It is an enlightened and thoughtful statement, describing the training process as a partnership, a shared experience between instructor and trainee, rather than as an imposed discipline. Doogan's long period as warden did much to help establish the special and distinctive Brathay atmosphere – busy, directed and conscientious, but also cheerful, considerate and relaxed in manner. It could be argued that Doogan had an enviable job: for the most part he was free to run Brathay his way – Scott trusted him to do it conscientiously – and there was the reassurance that the Scott Trust money would always be there to meet his needs. There was freedom to experiment and try new ideas. But the key factors – the wise choice of staff and the creation of a happy working atmosphere – sprang from Doogan's own abilities and personality. Recognition came in 1960 when a team of inspectors from the Ministry of Education came to look at Brathay. The Brathay keynotes, they reported, were self-discovery and enjoyment rather than self-conquest in the face of hazards. They pronounced the work 'admirably designed and organised to achieve its aims'.

The founder's intent

The four-week courses continued to be the staple of Brathay throughout the 1960s. Scott, by this time in his mid-80s but still vigorous, lively-minded and deeply concerned about all that went on at Brathay, regularly turned up for the theatre performance that marked the end of each four-week course. He was greeted like royalty and escorted to his seat in the front row. In November 1967 he wrote a summary of the Brathay experiment and called it *An Expression of Intent*.

The main purpose which, as original founder of the Trust, I had in view was the freedom to experiment (clear from any obligation to industry or any pressure from Public Authorities) among ideal surroundings provided by nature, in the opening of young minds to the opportunities for healthy and invigorating physical exertion, in learning to walk the hills with understanding use of map and compass, to gain rudimentary skill in sailing and rowing on the lake, and in elementary introduction to the visual arts and in dramatic representation.

All this experience would seem to be inadequate in opening and enlarging the windows of a boy's mind if it did not include the experience, almost certainly new to the average industrial boy, of living in a community, in loyalty to his dormitory team, and in the opportunity to show leadership on the expeditions and the general course activities. As an outcome, he will gain some experience of the discipline needed to take his place in the activities he takes part in. And while religion is not thrust at him, he will take part in simple morning and evening prayers as the normal life of the community.

These ideas will obviously demand a very real sense of dedication on the part of the staff, and they must never look upon the Centre as a career in itself, but as an experience to go through qualifying for wider responsibility elsewhere. Equally the aims of the founder will be incomplete in range if they do not include the inculcation and example by the staff in self-giving and in a real human interest in the individual personalities of the boys on the course. One of the most authentic tests of whether Brathay is living up to these ideals will be in these personal relationships between the Warden, the Staff and the boys.

THE SPIRITUAL DIMENSION

Scott makes specific mention in *An Expression of Intent* to 'simple morning and evening prayers' as part of the pattern of life at Brathay. In their formative years, Brathay, Outward Bound and Lindley Lodge all made clear reference to a spiritual basis in their work, and some retain this theme today. However, as Everard comments:

Nowadays, in our multicultural society, it is not so easy or so wise to attach an explicitly Christian label to Development Training and to offer the ritual of morning prayers. But no history would be complete without a recognition of the part that Christian values have played, and continue quietly to play, in interpreting the adventurous experiences that are at the heart of the Outward Bound approach.

The practice of morning and evening prayers at Brathay, gathering in the main hallway and facing the main door on which there was a wooden cross, was diligently upheld until the demise of the four-week courses in 1975. Although attendance was voluntary, in practice people did attend and accepted it as a part of the course. From the reports and comments of boys it was clear that this was a valued occasion; one that was used not for any indoctrination, but as an occasion when all could be invited to think about the wider dimensions of life. The old Army rule not to talk in the mess about religion certainly didn't apply at Brathay: what took place twice a day in the hallway was all of a piece with moving experiences in the hills or on the lake, or in the formal or informal reflections on what effect the four-week course was having on one's outlook on life. Prayers were taken by the duty instructor. To help him, and to provide a coherent and progressive pattern, a book of introductions, prayers and readings was produced in the 1950s together with a 'lightweight' version for the groups to use themselves when out camping. There was also an Exploration Group version that was used widely. The anthology of readings grew in the following decade and many of those readings and prayers, plus reflective writings by the boys themselves, were collected by Cameron Cochrane during his time as warden, and made into a presentation volume for Scott on his 90th birthday in 1971.

The religious opportunity was taken a step further in the early 1970s when for three years, Ware, with the support of Armstrong (by then retired nearby) and the local curate, arranged a Brathay Service each Sunday at 9.30 a.m. in the church built by Redmayne of Brathay Hall. People came in good numbers from all sections of Brathay and, in true Brathay manner, the service was something they prepared and ran themselves.

Has all this now been left behind? Certainly there is no explicit recognition or observance which, as Everard states, would be difficult to implement. But, if the work of Brathay is to encourage people to examine their lives, many will experience some spiritual awareness, however that may be defined, as a consequence, and this can only be enhanced by working in an environment that so many people in history have found to be spiritually uplifting.

THEME 3:
THE BRATHAY EXPLORATION GROUP

Of all the operations at Brathay, the work of the Brathay Exploration Group (BEG) is the one that has been least changed throughout the past half-century. This is both a tribute to the rightness of it as a concept, and to the devotion and enterprise of the many volunteer leaders who have sustained it throughout that time. The BEG pre-dates the four-week courses (see Theme 2), and grew out of the earliest of the Holidays with Purpose courses in 1947 (see Theme 1).

The following account is of a group of eight, pioneering a difficult route up a remote, heavily forested valley, in British Columbia in 1975.

Day Three
After an hour we reached more open ground, but there was much rockfall and caves: good bear country, but with not a trace of water. We were exhausted and periodic stops were becoming more necessary, with the subsequent restarts, lifting up the packs, progressively more agonising. But we had to keep going till we found water. It was now 8.30 p.m. and it's situations like this that make one feel like saying 'stop the expedition: I want to get off'. We plodded on while Al and Don went ahead. Then, at 9.15, back came the shout 'Water, quarter-mile ahead!'. The nicest words we ever heard. By the time the main group had got there, Al had got the fire going. It was a heavenly site and though darkness was fast approaching we set to and enjoyed one of the most appreciated meals of our lives. Two days later we reached the mountains and glaciers, and the main party, which had arrived by helicopter.

THE EARLY TARN SURVEYS

Tarn surveys were one of the many activities undertaken by people on the early BEG courses, and the following account is taken from the original report on their value.

Vaughan Lewis of the Geography Department at Cambridge University had told Brian Ware of his interest in obtaining information about the depths of Lake District tarns, particularly those lying in the great armchair-shaped hollows in the mountains. The almost complete lack of information was a serious obstacle to research into glacial erosion in the Lake District.

The challenge of this relatively simple but real task of exploration appealed to the first groups of boys from industry, and an expedition to Easedale Tarn was organised. Vaughan Lewis came up to help, and survey equipment was lent by Cambridge and the Freshwater Biological Association. A collapsible assault craft was used and a large number of soundings taken during a series of daily visits. The boys came from firms that included Dunlop, Mather & Platts, and Bibby, plus two boys from Windermere Grammar School. Later a Brathay group sounded Angle Tarn under Bowfell, and for this apprentices from Brockhouse Engineering Co. devised outriggers to go on a lightweight fighter pilot's dinghy to give it stability in these rougher waters. The daily journey up Rossett Gill was arduous and led to the decision that, in future, the group would camp at the mountain sites for the duration of a survey.

The success of that first year led to a more ambitious expedition to Blea Water. Jack Baiss, the leader, was another ex-Cambridge geographer. The party consisted of boys from the United Steel Co. at Workington, the National Coal Board, Chloride Electrical Storage Co., Richard Thomas & Baldwins, and Filtons (Aircraft), plus an equal number of boys from Hertford Grammar School and Merchant Taylors' School. From that time, the principle of recruiting boys equally from schools and industry became established. Also established was the principle of recruiting undergraduates as junior leaders; many of these later took on leadership and helped to run the group in other ways. Scientifically, the Blea Water expedition was notable in that it discovered the remarkable tarn depth of 207ft.

In 1949, with an increased demand for places, four tarn survey expeditions were run, each comprising 12–15 boys plus leaders. Charterhouse, Isleworth County School, Rugby and

Sounding Angle Tarn above Patterdale, 1952.

Uppingham schools and people from British Railways, Stewarts & Lloyds, and Telfers were involved, as well boys from the Oxford & Bermondsey Boys' Club. Life in mountain camps could be demanding, but much experience was gained. Equally important was maintaining a balance between the physical/social goals, and the scientific objectives. The purposes of each expedition could be readily understood, and it was the feeling of undertaking a piece of real exploration that caught the imagination and helped to lay the foundation for the Exploration Group. Some years later, a 16mm sound film was made recalling those early lake survey expeditions. It won an award as one of the Ten Best amateur films of the year and, as such, helped to spread news about the group very widely.

THE VOLUNTARY/PROFESSIONAL PARTNERSHIP

As an essentially voluntary body, BEG realised the importance of maintaining its own identity *vis-à-vis* the professional set-up within the mainstream Brathay operation based at the Hall. This they achieved first by obtaining the confidence of the professionals in the quality of the work the BEG was doing, which meant that those at Brathay could see them as useful partners in youth development despite their amateur status. Second, BEG obtained the backing of an independent council of people distinguished in the worlds of science and exploration. This council was not only able to consider and approve the plans and policies of the group, it was also active in bringing forward ideas for tasks to be undertaken, seeing that the work done was written up effectively and published, and taking responsibility for balancing the budget. The Scott trustees had been generous to the group in providing the hutted base in the woods (see later), and gave them a modest annual allowance for equipment and basic administration (typing, postage and reports). It was up to the group to cover all its running costs from the fees taken. Since many of the youngsters they aimed to take had limited means, this was quite a challenge. The group met it successfully, however, and only once, in the early days, accepted grant aid – from King George's Jubilee Trust and the Ministry of Education to establish a bank of camp equipment. Leaders shared in the expedition costs, usually paying at least half the full fee. Their contribution in skills and leadership was gratefully regarded by Brathay as BEG's input to the total Brathay operation. Thus the members of the group were seen as partners, despite the group's independence.

By 1950 BEG, now formally established, was running its expeditions independently of Holidays with Purpose. The group extended its programme of four lakes expeditions with an expedition to the Jotunheim mountains and glaciers of Norway. The work linked up naturally since, in Norway, they were mapping real glaciers of the kind that once occupied those Lakeland tarns. The work was done in association with Cambridge Glaciological Research Project in the same area, but with Brathay producing its own, valued, results. The people who went to Norway were picked from those who had previously done a lakes expedition, thus setting a pattern of continuity that was to be the basis of the group for many years. The pattern had the dual advantage of ensuring that the people going overseas were well trained and acquainted with 'Brathay's ways'. It also ensured that there was a good flow of people through the lakes expeditions, which provided the basic training ground.

THE BASE IN THE WOODS

By 1951 the group had outgrown the Hall accommodation and, after a summer based in tents in the grounds, it moved in 1952 into a new 20-bed hutted headquarters in the woods. There was still a strong link with the Hall since one of the trustees, John Trevelyan, became the first chairman of the Brathay Exploration Group Committee. Equally important was the arrangement made with the Hall about the intake of members. The main work at the Hall was now four-week courses for industrial apprentices, and it was agreed that every year outstanding boys would be recommended for a place on a BEG expedition. In many cases, because of their Brathay training, these boys could go straight into an overseas trip. Thus began an important link between the two arms of Brathay that was to do so much to enhance the reputation of both over the coming decades.

Life in the new huts was not without drama. In August 1953, on the first evening of an expedition, having left the heating stove in the dormitory safely damped down, the group members all went down to the Hall for a film show. An hour later the hut was a blazing inferno. The next day, the insurance assessor traced the cause to a construction fault and immediate action was taken to get a replacement hut. Brathay lent clothes to the boys, but the expedition to Blea Water went on as planned. When they returned from the mountains a new hut had just arrived and the last two days were spent with one group of nine erecting the hut and the other group in the Brathay studio working up the survey results. Despite the loss of the hut and much personal gear, the boys had shown remarkable team spirit throughout these 10 traumatic days. Brian Ware said: 'It was a privilege to lead such a party'.

The growth of the Brathay Exploration Group over the following 20 years was the consequence of carefully developing an established and successful pattern of work. Based in the hutted headquarters, there would be four 10-day expeditions in the summer and two seven-day expeditions at Easter, all in the Lake District and all at low cost with low overheads. Once the tarn surveys were complete, the group went on to do a whole series of other useful field surveys, ranging from studies of lake temperatures, peat, moraines, land-use, old mines, and estuaries, to acid rain, frogspawn and the number of tourists climbing Helvellyn.

The original Exploration Group huts, built in 1952.

The headquarters in the woods went through several stages of evolution. In 1964 they put up the dormitory block, with two 'sides' to it plus leaders' bays. This anticipated future use by mixed groups. The new dormitory freed the old hut to become an equipment store, much needed because until then most of the kit had been stored in an old converted water tank at the Hall. The equipment store was the focus of much care and maintenance by a succession of volunteers, who would often spend many weeks on this essential work. In 1969, a bright and well-designed common room block was added, enabling rather more than the basic 20 to be accommodated in the headquarters. This was necessary because it was increasingly common for groups going elsewhere in the world to have a preliminary meet at the huts.

REPORTS

One responsibility of a group that claims to be doing useful original survey work is to see that the results of its work are in fact used. In most cases this means passing them on to others or at least publishing reports. The BEG has set a shining example in this respect, diligently filing reports from the earliest days. By the autumn, every leader was required to produce a first report, which was duplicated and sent out to all members before Christmas. This helped people to know what was going on and how their own work fitted into the larger pattern. Later came the printed annual report, with a summary of all the scientific work. Every year, the major expeditions would also produce their own reports, sometimes with extended facts on all the fieldwork done.

Over the years, the volume of work produced in this way has been considerable (a summary of the group's publications is given in Appendix F). Between 1953 and 1985, some 75 individual expedition reports were produced, all designed to inform a wider public of their research. There were also some 119 smaller field reports contained within the annual reports, plus the reports that appeared in other journals or publications, of which there were at least 72, including articles in the *Geographical Magazine,* the *Times Educational Supplement,* and the *Uganda Journal.*

Perhaps the most widespread use of BEG surveys was within the schools' series *Longmans Study Geography.* Studies of communities and geography in Foula, Norway and Iceland formed the basis of chapters in these books which, over the years, sold almost a million copies in the UK as well as in many countries abroad.

The work of the group has also been documented in 10 films, mostly 16mm colour sound productions made by Explorer Films, the author's company, and these have had the further aim of showing others how to run similar expeditions.

Digging an ice tunnel.

THE EXPEDITIONS

Foula

From 1956, a whole sequence of expeditions began to the remote Shetland island of Foula. Thanks to the co-operation of the laird, Brathay was able to reconstruct a derelict croft house and in effect establish a second base from which two or three expeditions were run every year for the next 27 years. The scientific work in Foula was mainly ornithological, ringing and studying the prolific bird colonies, and around this work grew up a coterie of leaders known as Bird Men. But there was another side to the Foula work. Life on the UK's remotest inhabited island is bleak and the islanders can be cut off for many weeks at a time in winter. A visit by a dozen youngsters was welcome, and they could also provide much-needed practical support such as lifting the peat, assisting in the sheep round-ups, or even just stopping for a chat. The Brathay group even took responsibility for running the kirk service when the minister was away. Brathay took all this in its stride, and there can be no doubt of the lasting impact on the many hundreds of individuals who were lucky enough to visit Foula. In modern terms, when it wasn't ringing birds, what the BEG was doing in Foula was community service, and so began a practice which, like the expeditions themselves, has now become commonplace.

Overseas expeditions

After the Lake District groups and the Foula groups, the third 'layer' of Brathay expeditions was the overseas ventures. Like the other layers, these were mostly part of a carefully built-up pattern in which, once a routine was established, leaders could pass on their skills to their successors without much central control. Norway featured regularly, to which one or two countries a year were added until 1962, when the programme included Norway, Iceland, Tunisia and Uganda.

Every January from 1951, there was another key event: the leaders' New Year meeting in Brathay Hall. This was not just a reunion but essential to planning, so important in an organisation that had no central administration of its own other than Ware's telephone. Over three very busy days, broken only by the chance of a brisk afternoon walk, between 50 and 100 members of the BEG would gather to hear proud but none-too-serious accounts of the previous year's expeditions, debate one or two fundamental issues, and then get down to plans for the coming year. Importantly, there would also be a slot on the first evening for the warden to speak of what had been going on in the Hall, the parent body of the group, and events would usually end with a social.

Iceland 1953

In 1953 the Exploration Group prepared to mount an expedition to the volcanic mountains and glaciers of Iceland. Such an activity might sound commonplace today, but this was one of the very first young people's expeditions to venture this far at the time. From 1932, the dominant group in the world of schools' expeditions had been the British Schools Exploring Society (BSES), formerly the Public Schools' Exploring Society, which annually ran one big expedition of around 50 or 60 boys, and had a strong 'services' tradition in its leadership. But there was little else on offer to young people, and nothing for those without a sixth-form background. Brathay was not only opening expeditions to a wider clientele in terms of social background, it also aimed to keep costs as low as possible so that people were not put off by the expense.

Each of the 12 members (leaders and boys) paid £30, which covered all travel expenses, food, insurance and camping equipment – all the costs of the trip. Assiduous cadging helped to keep the costs down: Selfridges provided miscellaneous groceries; Rowntrees gave chocolate and cocoa; Bovril supplied the vital pemmican; Tate & Lyle gave them sugar; and Romney's of Kendal presented the Kendal Mint Cake. (The following year Romney's proudly proclaimed that their product had been used by three notable groups: Colonel Hunt's successful Everest expedition, Cambridge University in Norway, and the Brathay Exploration Group!)

The leaders approached leading Icelandic scientists for their suggestions on useful projects since, like all Brathay expeditions, the aim was to do original work. Eventually projects were planned and all was ready, and the group sailed from Leith on 10 August. After a very rough passage, steerage, to Reykjavik, the group was dismayed at the prices: 'We found everything very dear,' one of the apprentices reported. 'One and sixpence [was] the average price for a cup of tea.' A coach took them along rough roads to the edge of the Langjokull ice-cap, more than 50 miles north-east of Reykjavik. Here they set up their base camp close to a stream in a small area of rough grass and dwarf bilberries. The closest human habitation was a farm two hours' rough walking away.

The first task was to set up a sub-camp near the summit of Ok, a remnant ice-cap straddling the crater of an extinct volcano some 4000ft above base camp. The ascent was often in thick mist and driving sleet, first over fields of boulders and then up interminable snow slopes. The top camp was established on 15 August, a single tent just inside the rim of the crater.

The next task was to dig a tunnel horizontally into the snow and ice of the glacier just below the rim. This tunnel was some 40ft long and was, in effect, a 'junior partner' to the 300 foot tunnel that Cambridge had dug in Norway in order to study the layers in the ice and the contact with the back wall. The BEG tunnel also had a second purpose: somewhere to go if the tent blew away! Following this, the team then surveyed the half-mile wide crater, using the plane table to plot the layout. Frequent bad weather with minimal visibility did much to hamper their progress. But they pressed doggedly on, taking it in turns to occupy the top camp in two-man teams.

Uganda

The range of work undertaken by the group grew steadily wider, extending to studies of mountain landscapes in what was then Yugoslavia and the Pyrenees (1958) and archaeology in Tunisia (1962). The Uganda expedition of 1962 also introduced the idea of partnership with young people in the country visited. Thanks to good school links, the group recruited an almost equal number of Ugandan schoolboys, and going into the remoter regions, the tropical forests, and the deserts was just as much a novel experience for them as it was for the pale-kneed Englishmen. The trip caught the national imagination as it was filmed by the BEG and later shown by the BBC as part of David (now Sir David) Attenborough's *Adventure* series. Of the African members of this expedition one later became vice-chancellor of Nairobi University and another Minister of Health in Kenya.

It is often the silly, smaller incidents that stick in the memory. One member of the Ugandan trip recalls the constant screech of the cicadas outside and hearing an earnest discussion between two boys, one English, one Ugandan, as he sat in his hut one dark evening. They were hotly debating the precise meaning of the word 'apposite', and this after a day when they had been trudging up the slopes of one of Africa's largest volcanoes, in a very 'long line of everybody', porters and all.

On another African expedition, this time in Tunisia, there is the story of the Brathay expedition coming across and assisting a party stranded in the desert. It turned out that this 'party' comprised the naturalist Julian Huxley, and Dr Max Nicholson, director general of the Nature Conservancy! They were glad of the help which, one said to the other, 'was all part of the Brathay service!'.

Expansion

Throughout the 1960s, the group took a total of some 200 people on between 13 and 17 expeditions each year. Destinations included Poland (then a mysterious place behind the Iron Curtain), Greenland and Kenya, as well as a wide range of BEG expedition opportunities in Scotland, Wales and Ireland. (See Appendix D for a complete list.) These were developed for a variety of reasons. Many people who applied for overseas expeditions were not yet sufficiently skilled, but perhaps thought that the Lake District might be too 'tame'. For them these expeditions offered a useful intermediate level of challenge. Also, these UK expeditions were reasonably low-cost, although more expensive than the huts-based Lake District ones. As with all

other BEG expeditions in the early days and mid-period, there was always a firm base of worthwhile field work tasks, often linked in to the needs of universities or bodies such as the Nature Conservancy. Despite the expansion, the six or seven Lake District expeditions each year remained at the core of the BEG operations.

LINKS WITH MAINSTREAM BRATHAY

The strength of purpose and the enthusiasm of the BEG are indicated by the fact that its members were behind the establishment of the Brathay Field Study Centre in Old Brathay in 1967 (see Theme 4). With the resources and the staff of the Field Study Centre to support them, the next decade saw further expansion, with numbers often well into the 300s and up to 20 expeditions.

Unfortunately, with the decline in industrial apprenticeships combined with shorter courses at the Hall, there was no longer the same flow of people moving on to the BEG after a Brathay Hall course. This was partly compensated for by boys from Project Trident (see Theme 6) and from people attending the Field Centre. In 1969, the Field Centre link led to Tony Land having a joint role as BEG secretary. A keen geographer and ornithologist, he had been involved with the group for more than 10 years, taking part in many expeditions. He now joined the centre staff and shared his time between BEG work and tutoring field courses. This was the first time in 22 years that the BEG had had a paid officer – until then Ware, with some typing assistance, had carried the major burden, supported by a schools secretary (Jack Baiss and later Tony Land), an industry secretary (Alan Barrett at Brathay Hall) and a membership secretary.

In 1971, Land returned to Uppingham School and his place was taken by Bob Metcalfe, who, after a deputy headship in Scotland, subsequently went on to become head of the YMCA Centre at Lakeside at the south end of Windermere. That YMCA link has come full circle since John Naylor, another former principal of that centre, became chairman of the BEG trustees in 1996 in succession to Ware. In 1978, links became even closer when a merger formed the Centre for Exploration and Field Studies, under the direction (from 1979) of Michael Gee (see Theme 4).

In the 1980s, BEG entered a period of uncertainty about its role. What had begun as a unique experience for young people was now, thanks to the expansion of opportunities, commonplace. Going abroad was no longer an adventure in itself, and to the sophisticated youngster the Lake District was old hat. A great many schools and youth organisations were running their own expeditions, and individuals could sign up for challenging opportunities from the Duke of Edinburgh's Award to Operations Drake and Raleigh. Although many of the BEG leaders could claim some of the credit for this expansion, the reaction within the group was to turn in upon itself and seek to work around the needs of its membership. For a time they considered dropping field studies and aligning themselves with the development training objectives of the mainstream professional Brathay operation. Then, in 1988, after a survey of needs, BEG decided that the future lay in an independent set-up within the campus of Brathay. Part of the reason for wanting independence was a fear that management at Brathay was no longer supporting work with young people, as indicated by a drop in the number of under-25s attending the professionally-led courses as a proportion of all-comers from 90% to 28%.

The embrace of the Field Study Centre in the 1970s was, in the long run, a mixed blessing. It brought the support of a salaried secretary, which greatly improved the working efficiency of the group, but once a 'professional' is in place, there is a tendency for the volunteers to sit back and leave much of the work to that person (as Charles Folland, Christine Clephan and Steve Dickinson, the successors at the helm of BEG discovered). And, of course, a professional must be paid, which proved to be quite a drain on the modest finances of the group. Besides these higher costs, inflation, cutbacks in schools, and general recession had a severe effect on the BEG. The option of returning to a self-governing status was attractive. Going independent meant losing the administrative surcharge put on it by Brathay, but it also meant a swing back to a largely voluntary way of working, backed only by the hard work of one 'retired' professional, Ron Barrow.

It now looks as if the tide has turned. The BEG is once again an independent group, its story since 1992, like that of the Hall itself, being one of steady recovery. From a decline in numbers to under 100, by 1995 it had returned to over 200 a year. While there has been no progress on re-establishing Lake District expeditions, the overseas work has been impressive. In 1995 there were nine overseas expeditions with a record 141 participants. There were expeditions to China, Kenya, the Amazon, Lappland, Norway, the Alps, and Bulgaria. Training is now an important feature and there are regular leadership courses in Scotland and first aid courses in the Lakes. At 3903, the 'delegate day' score was the highest since 1983, although still well below the 1975 peak of 6006. It is the group's intention to develop the Lake District base as a clubhouse and centre for work in partnership with other organisations, the principal one being Brathay Hall itself.

THE WIDER INFLUENCE OF THE BRATHAY EXPLORATION GROUP

In March 1988, there was a gathering at the Royal Geographical Society to celebrate 40 years of growth by the Brathay Exploration Group. It was not just an inward-looking occasion. Apart from its own successes, one of the most notable features about the group has been the way it has led the way for others in the world of youth exploration. The 40th anniversary meeting considered the following to be the main lessons learnt or benefits offered by the BEG.

- BEG leaders were quite often schoolmasters, and when they had seen what was possible, many of them went back and ran their own school expeditions. Even BEG members got bitten by this bug. An early example was John Longland who, two years after his Brathay Iceland expedition, was running his own peer group expedition to that country. The reports from boys who had also been on Hall courses show that many of them had gained the confidence to venture out on their own soon afterwards. This was a brave thing to do in those early days when travel was not so easy.
- By doing real research, the BEG demonstrated that under proper guidance, young people could produce results that were useful and acceptable for universities and research bodies. The best official recognition in the early days came in an article in the prestigious science magazine *Nature*. In 'The Amateur Scientist in Britain', R.G. Brightman gives generous coverage to an account of Brathay's survey work and concludes '...without the help of the amateur scientists, the prosecution of research...into problems of ornithology, meteorology and...ecology would be impossible'. One distinguished scientist who worked on Brathay expeditions frequently made particular mention of the fact that having a mixture of schoolboys and apprentices was most beneficial. Whereas the schoolboy might have a theory about some task, it was often the practical experience of the apprentice that made things happen.
- Besides its reports on expeditions, the BEG produced other publications, such as *Prayers for Use on Expeditions* (1965). Although intended as an internal handbook, it achieved a surprising success amongst other youth groups, particularly the Boys' Brigade. Some years later, BEG member Dr Robin Illingworth produced *Expedition Medicine, a Planning Guide*, which received wide acclaim and extensive use.
- In 1971, the BEG encapsulated much of its expedition experience in the *Handbook for Expeditions*. This work covered not only the logistics of expedition planning and the particular problems and responsibilities of youth leadership, but it also had extensive advice on all the various kinds of field investigations that are appropriate for young groups. These chapters were all written by specialist leaders in the group. Its success led to a double-sized sequel, *The Expedition Handbook*, in 1978.
- In 1971, the BEG and the British Schools' Exploring Society decided to form an association of the main youth exploring bodies so that their experience could be made more widely available. Consequently, following a meeting at Old Brathay, and under the auspices of the Royal Geographical Society, the Young Explorers' Trust (YET) was born. A great many of the leading participants were BEG leaders who were turning their skills to the wider field. Among the most prominent must be Tony Escritt, a master from Harrow. Having set high standards on Brathay expeditions, he now set about making himself 'Mr Iceland' by forming the Iceland Unit of the YET. In that role he has brought countless expeditions into the world of

exploration and established strong links with the Icelandic authorities.

- The YET and the Royal Geographical Society were co-founders of the Expedition Advisory Centre, which rapidly grew to become the major information and training source for small expeditions. Their annual seminar handbook *Running a Small Expedition*, can be seen as the direct successor of Brathay's early *Handbook for Expeditions*.
- The field quarters of the BEG, the huts, have themselves been of great benefit to those wishing to follow in BEG's footsteps. Some schools, usually those whose staff have Brathay connections, regularly use them as a base for their own school exploits in the Lake District, usually running weeks with a blend of adventure and field studies. Those huts were also the base for two Brathay Hall enterprises, the Trident Trust courses and the work in intermediate treatment.
- Films of BEG expeditions was the start of Explorer Films. This company used Brathay experience to produce outdoor training films on hillcraft (and other activities) that became the staple diet for schools and youth organisations for the following two decades. The successor on video, *Hillcraft*, is now a core material for the Duke of Edinburgh's Award.
- The early BEG experience can be seen as one of the influences leading to the 1986 Windsor Conference on Outdoor Adventure and Challenge for Youth. The conference commissioned a study that led to the publication in 1989 of the Hunt report, *In Search of Adventure*, with its advocacy of the right of all young people to have the opportunity of some challenging outdoor experience. This aim is now being taken forward by a national body, the Foundation for Outdoor Adventure. The first publication from that body is *Why Adventure?*, a very wide survey of the research literature on the role and value of outdoor adventure in young people's personal and social development, co-authored by Roger Greenaway, a former member of the Brathay staff.

The spirit, aims and rationale of the BEG seem to be well caught by the following paragraph taken from *The Adventure Alternative* (Colin Mortlock, 1984).

To climb, sail, canoe, or journey in a hazardous environment in a self-reliant manner may seem a dangerous and unjustifiable extravagance in a modern world. Nothing could be further from the truth, for life is a paradox. Society desperately needs young people who are determined and courageous. Young people are the most valuable resource in the world – the citizens of tomorrow. When they go on a demanding outdoor journey they are displaying the exploring instinct common to all living things. And in common with all other forms of life on the planet it is both natural and traditional for that journey to be dangerous and uncertain.

And the remembered pleasure of it all. The first Brathay expedition to the North American wilderness in 1975 trod in the steps of pioneer explorer Howard Palmer. This account, which Palmer wrote in 1912, is an appropiate end to the chapter on BEG.

Our last camp occupied the loveliest spot of all, the tip of a narrow island in the main channel. At dusk we lolled about the fire, watching the ruddy sunset glow, which suffused the distant summits and filmy clouds above and was painted again in the smoothly speeding waters at our feet. The weariness of the battle was in our bones and the memory of toils fresh, yet who will deny that such evenings make up for all? Bestowed unexpectedly as a fresh gift from Nature's bounty, they cast a magic spell over whatever of hardship and discouragement has gone before, transmuting all later recollections into the sweetest one can know.

THEME 4:
THE FIELD STUDY CENTRE

Field studies make a departure from education based wholly on transmitted learning in that they provide abundant means by which students may learn through observation. Ideally, educational field work should continue through the whole of a child's school life. If it did so the curiosity of the child and his joy in the world of nature would never end abruptly as they so often do, but would lead in later youth to a critical interest in his environment and a capacity to gain reliable and usable knowledge from what he sees around him.

G.E. Hutchings' presidential address to the Geographical Association, 1962

Sell off Old Brathay to a university? In 1965, the leaders of the Brathay Exploration Group (BEG) were alarmed when they heard that there was a possibility of Old Brathay being lost. Since the demise of the Oxfordshire courses in 1958 (see Theme 6), the second major building on the campus had reverted to its former role as a conference centre, although in practice there had not been a lot of use of it for that purpose. After discussion at the BEG leaders' meeting, Brian Ware, still at that time at Uppingham School and still honorary secretary of the BEG, set about preparing a proposal for a Field Study Centre.

This was a time when people were growing increasingly concerned about environmental issues, especially pollution, and the adverse effects on the natural world of technological advances. The Lake District had recently been declared a National Park, as an area in need of special protection. As a widely-travelled geographer, Ware was conscious of the dangers, the complexity of the problems, and the urgent need for increased environmental awareness. He had served on the Nature Conservancy's 'Science Out of Doors' working party. He knew that the Field Studies Council and education authorities were setting up field study centres in various places, although there was no proposal for one in the Lake District.

He submitted his ideas to the Brathay Hall management committee. The Lake District, he argued, was an admirable location for field studies in many subjects. Brathay had the facilities, at Old Brathay, and the experience and contacts through the BEG. 'Brathay's experience over the past 15 years and its wide contacts in industry and schools could be used to set up a pioneer Field Study Centre with an adventurous background,' he wrote.

The proposal was enthusiastically welcomed by Francis Scott, who was a keen naturalist and vice-president of the Cumbria Wildlife Trust, by the Brathay trustees, and by their chairman, the Right Reverend Mervyn Armstrong, Bishop of Jarrow. Early in 1965 the BEG council set up a sub-committee, comprising Professor J.A. Steers, John Kempe and Professor Gordon Manley, to make plans for the programme, staffing, equipment and links with the BEG. Armstrong looked at the finances, and he and Steers secured the support of the Dulverton, Pilgrim and Leverhulme Trusts to cover staff costs for the first three years.

The Brathay trustees decided that the new arrangements (with the Brathay operation now consisting of the Hall courses, the Field Study Centre and the Exploration Group) called for the appointment of one overall 'head'. So it was that, in January 1966, the trustees invited Ware, who had been involved in all the planning stages, to become the first director of Brathay (later to be redesignated principal), with the initial task of establishing the new Field Study Centre. He took up his duties in August 1966. Ware's wife, Marjorie, supervised the catering and housekeeping at the field centre and for Brathay as a whole for more than a decade, making sure that high standards were maintained and that cheerful hospitality was offered to all visitors. In 1969 Low Brathay, a new house near Old Brathay, was provided for them.

Although the idea seemed to go beyond the original intentions of the Brathay Trust ('... for the education ... of young persons ... *from industry* ...'), Scott was fully supportive and threw himself into the creation of a first class Field Study Centre. He made a generous donation from his own personal money for the building of the Francis Scott Laboratory, and, again at his own expense, presented the centre with a top quality microscope. As for the environmental concerns, Scott was able to remind the trustees that it was for this that he had purchased the Brathay estate in the first place.

The first task was to convert Old Brathay to take 24 students and up to six visiting staff. They would offer one-week courses – Wednesday to Wednesday – to sixth form students of both sexes working towards A-level examinations in geography or biology. The students' teachers would often accompany them and help the Brathay staff. The courses would be intensive and relevant, directly related to the living landscape. In this way environmental issues would be brought alive and made real.

The Field Study Centre opened for business in March 1967. Initially, Ware acted as director of studies until a replacement could be found to release him for his prime role as principal. Ware recalls:

We found just the right man for the job in Mike Mortimer, who had worked for the past 16 years with the Game and Fisheries Department in Zambia. He was a biologist and had become their Chief Fisheries Officer. He was rugged and tough, highly practical and enthusiastic. He took over in February 1968 and gathered around him a first class staff of young graduates, including biologist Rod Young and geographer John Barkham. The staff made a great success of the courses and soon began to gain a high reputation. In a way we were being too successful, and some schools grew almost too dependent upon us.

But the success was not just in straight learning:

Many headmasters and teachers said their students were coming back from Brathay with a totally different view. They had begun to understand what science was all about. It was no longer just a classroom subject.

Few records remain to describe the experiences of students first hand, but the following extract from the very first brochure records Brathay's aspirations for the course, which by all accounts were matched by the reality.

The Brathay estate, with its extensive woods and parklands, is ideally situated for field studies. For over a mile the River Brathay, with interesting variations in gradient and volume, forms the northern boundary before flowing into Windermere. There are one and a half miles of lake shore varying from rocky headlands to delta, fen and sandy bays. Geologically the situation is particularly interesting because Brathay lies at the junction of the Borrowdale volcanic series and the Silurian slates, flags and grits, a narrow band of Coniston limestone outcropping between them and running right across the estate. There is ready access to a wide variety of mountain scenery, both in the immediate vicinity on foot or further afield using the centre's own transport.

COURSES

Sixth form courses; geography and biology

For boys and girls studying for A-level examinations. The courses are planned and implemented by the staff but visiting staff are encouraged to take an active part.

A tutorial approach is adopted and there will normally not be more than 12 students in a teaching group. Emphasis is placed upon enquiry and intelligent thinking, and students are encouraged to examine critically their own observations and to draw conclusions from them. Practical involvement is considered more important than passive acceptance of instruction. Whenever possible students are given an opportunity to participate in long-term field research projects.

The geography course has as its primary aim the study of the evolution of the Lake District landscape, with particular reference to glaciation and the impact of man. Students are introduced to basic field techniques, including elementary surveying, the examination of soil profiles and the study of vegetation.

The biology course is essentially ecological and the main aim is to introduce students to the concept of environmental variation and habitat differences and to the techniques used to study their effect on plant and animal populations. Attention is given to the recognition of major groups of animals and plants.

Both the geography and biology courses have three further aims in common. Firstly, to draw attention to the fundamental principles and problems of planning field observations, and the recording, retrieval and interpretation of data. Secondly, to indicate to students the interdependence of geographical and biological studies. Thirdly, to provide the opportunity for students to plan and carry out projects of their own.

The Francis Scott Laboratory was completed in 1968. Besides schools, the field centre facilities were made available to universities and teacher training colleges to run their own courses, which were planned to fill in gaps in the programme of sixth-form courses, and to allow the residential tutorial staff to take holiday and study breaks, while making the fullest use of the centre's facilities. In practice, the regular contacts with university staff proved to be of great value. In the first full year, courses were attended by 439 school students and 140 from universities and training colleges. In the second full year (1969), there were about 60% more students, and 35 one-week courses, plus other special courses.

From 1969, the Old Brathay accommodation was expanded to take 36 students and up to eight visiting staff. This was done by making available the two dormitory blocks on the hill by the Francis Scott Laboratory. Both these dormitories had originally been built to accommodate training course groups. One was now converted into a run of two-bed cubicles, thus greatly increasing the flexibility of the accommodation. The other dormitory became the geography laboratory. The extra accommodation made it possible to accommodate up to 1250 students a year, which would give a potential of 8750 delegate days, a total reached by 1970.

Within the main building was established the John Doogan Library, named in memory of a much loved and remembered warden, all the more fitting because Old Brathay had been his home before the construction of Brathay Knott. Many generous gifts, including long runs of important scientific journals, soon enabled the library to become a really useful asset.

The centre had its own impressive advisory committee. Its chairman was Steers, recently retired from his post as Professor of Geography at Cambridge University. He had originally joined as the nominee of the Nature Conservancy and had taken an increasingly active role in Brathay's work since the tragic death of his colleague Vaughan Lewis in a car accident in 1961. His committee included senior academics from the universities of Lancaster, Newcastle and Leicester, and leading Lake District authorities. Practical projects undertaken by the centre, often in association with the BEG, included studies into the effects of mounting tourist pressure on the Lake District landscape, the erosion of fellside paths, and monitoring pollution and its impact on wildlife.

From the first there was close co-operation between the Field Study Centre and the BEG. Mortimer went to Foula with the BEG in 1967 and 1968 to work out a series of possible research topics, such as the ecology of the island, diseases among domestic animals, and the population of the Great Skua colony. It was seminal work and Foula was regarded as a kind of outstation of the Field Study Centre. In 27 consecutive seasons between 1956 and 1982, Brathay parties collected an enormous amount of information about the bird colonies and other matters, which led to the publication of *The Birds of Foula* and *The Flora of Foula* besides a great many other reports.

From its inception in 1967, the Field Study Centre was fully co-educational. This may seem natural enough now but, despite the clear statement in the original Trust deed that Brathay's prime purpose was 'the physical training and moral, intellectual and physical development of young persons *of both sexes*', no girls had ever actually attended the basic four-week courses. In 1969, all this changed. Ware says:

It was now that Brathay ceased to be all male. The Field Study Centre held mixed courses and the idea spread to the other wings of Brathay. We wondered why it had taken us so long to admit them.

As a consequence, from 1969 one four-week course a year was open to girls, and from 1976 it was 'open house' on all courses. The Hall appointed its first female tutor, Lyn Hayball, a drama

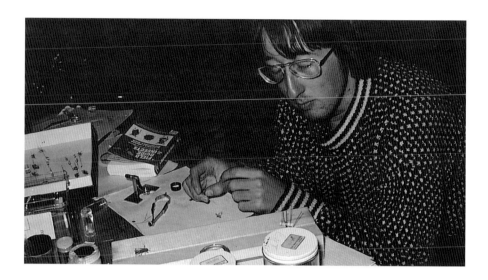

specialist, in 1971. In the BEG it was the 1970 'Summer Lakes III' and a Foula expedition that became the first British expeditions to take girls. In 1972, six out of 16 expeditions were open to girls, and by the following year there was no discrimination at all.

On any Brathay course the most important question is what effect it had on the participants. Did it change their lives? We can get some idea of how participants felt about the Field Study Centre from the letters sent by participating schools and colleges, some extracts from which follow.

The courses have always been well organised, the content valid and relevant to the life and needs of the students. More importantly, it was seen by ourselves as an opportunity for young adults to be in an environment away from home surrounded by people with different skills, experiences and backgrounds. Indeed, for many students it was their first opportunity to be away from parental supervision.

Our girls and boys gained a tremendous amount from the week – techniques in geography, mixing with pupils from other schools and the delight of living in the Lake District. It was particularly fascinating to see how a group of individuals moved from being a peculiar lot, to a team that could undertake and complete a task.

The courses are also valued for the development of personal and social skills. Students learn to work individually and in groups and develop a sense of responsibility to themselves and to others. This aspect of the field course is considered of equal importance to the academic work and, from our experience, is not always catered for adequately elsewhere.

I have seen the course develop over the years into one that is innovative and highly adaptive to suit most schools' requirements. There is no doubt in our minds that our students' A-level results have been enhanced as a direct result of participation in your excellent, thought provoking and wide-ranging course. The whole atmosphere in which the work occurs is different from that which we have, of necessity, to provide in school, and I feel it is a most valuable 'half-way house' for many between the world of school and work or university.

They appreciate and respond to the informality of Brathay teaching and, dare I suggest, probably get through far more work and learn far more than they would in two or even three weeks of work in school – or in many other field centres!

Every year I have taken a group up to Brathay I have been amazed by the transformation in each of my students, achieved over a single week. In the first tutor group sessions the students have to have even the simplest facts and ideas dragged out of them. They are quite content to be spoon-fed and have little or no idea how to organise themselves or how to work with others. Used to soft centrally-heated homes – and classrooms – they have no notion of how to cope with the cold, wind and rain that the Lake District can give them or how to see even easy tasks through to a logical conclusion. A week at Brathay soon puts an end to these weaknesses. By the end of courses, pupils are eagerly answering up, confident that it is better to make an offering and perhaps be proved wrong, than to say or do nothing at all. They have learnt to work with other students from sometimes very different areas, schools and backgrounds to achieve a common aim and justifiably take pride in having succeeded.

Because of the quality of the work, numbers attending courses in the early 1970s were encouragingly high. Between 1970 and 1975, the field centre had more delegate days per year than the courses at the Hall, and if one adds in the BEG figures, the two 'environmental' arms accounted for 63% of Brathay's total business. In 1971, more than 2000 people attended Brathay courses, but only 400 of these were on 'Hall' courses, the other 1600 were with either the field studies or the exploration groups. Such was the popularity of the centre, that little marketing was needed. Repeat business was the norm, and the allocation of places for the whole season was completed by March or earlier each year.

EXPANSION PLANS

Because of its popularity, between 1973 and 1975 some 500 more people wanted to attend the centre each year than there were places, and this prompted plans for expansion. The number of places had already grown from the original 24 to 40, and it was now proposed that this be increased to the 'more economic' 65. At the same time, it was suggested that the range of courses be increased to cover 'the study of the environment and concern for problems of conservation'. Courses for adults as well as young people were proposed, and there was to be greater emphasis on studying more aspects of the Lake District such as the geology, archaeology (including industrial archaeology), architecture, and the Lake poets and artists. There was already a good foundation for this development in the liaison the field study group had with other organisations, as outlined by the development proposal:

The centre has developed a close liaison with...the National Park Special Planning Board, the Nature Conservancy Council, the National Trust, the Forestry Commission and the Freshwater Biological Association. Rainfall records are kept for the North-West River Authority at a number of upland stations and at Brathay itself. There is a particularly close association with the Cumbria Naturalists' Trust. It is intended that the Naturalists' Trust's headquarters shall be established at the enlarged Brathay Centre, which will also be the base for its ambitious educational programme...The fine collection of Lepidoptera of the late Canon Hervey is housed at the centre and there is an excellent herbarium of Lake District plants...both available for consultation.

A move forward of this nature, however imaginative and well thought out, requires considerable investment, and the mid-1970s, with rising unemployment, was not the time for such developments. However, out of the proposals came one new scheme, to expand Brathay's provision for young people. It began in 1976 and involved the barn, the large building next to the Field Study Centre. An imaginative plan to convert this dilapidated farm building had already been submitted by Robert Gilchrist, Brathay's architect and for years an active member of the BEG. This would provide new bunk rooms, a splendid large assembly room plus an improved drying room.

The scheme would normally have been too expensive to contemplate, but thanks to the government's new Job Creation Scheme it was possible to plan the work so that it could be done very economically. There was also the opportunity to give employment training, in close liaison with the Construction Industry Training Board, for up to 12 young unemployed craftsmen. The construction firm Laings made a generous grant and agreed to manage the whole project, providing two skilled supervisors and a workforce of 12 unemployed trainees. The young trainees would live at Brathay, do a Brathay course for all-round personal development, and have two Manpower Services Commission-funded Brathay tutors seconded to organise activities for their out-of-work hours and weekends. A chance meeting between Ware and John Huskins, an inspector for the Youth Service, led to a Department of Education and Science grant of some £40,000, amounting to 50% of the total project price. The Francis Scott Trust also made a significant contribution.

The work took much longer than expected, mainly because the seconded trainees kept getting 'real' jobs, meaning that the contractors had to find new people each time. It was finally completed in the spring of 1978, and officially opened by Albert Booth, the Minister for Employment. The success of this conversion through a Job Creation Project attracted the Prince of Wales' (Drapers' Trust) Award and Grant to Brathay.

By 1977, the Field Study Centre had had 10 years of successful running with well-booked courses for most of that time. The 1977 season began on 19 January and ran through to 14 December, with 40 one-week courses running back to back except for a one-week break in June plus four other short periods totalling 14 days. Between March and October, the average occupancy of the 42 available beds was about 95%, which was very high. For four winter months, it was not possible to run field courses, but the time was used profitably for research and preparation.

Most of the work was the regular biology or geography courses; a combined nine-day geography/biology course was tried, but unsuccessfully. The standard size of teaching groups for all A-level work was 12. About 20–30% of the courses were run by universities and colleges, and there was a wide range of other meetings, courses and conferences, mostly of science groups but including a course for wardens of outdoor centres, and the annual teachers' courses of the Department of Education and Science. The place was also used for Brathay's own mainstream work: the St Helens Intermediate Treatment children used the field equipment and laboratories, and Union International Ltd held four management courses in which, as a project, they designed and built stiles for the Brathay estate. This reflected the growing interest of the field centre in making full use of the 350 acres within its boundaries. The staff even prepared a comprehensive Estate Management Plan for its development in the best interests of all users. In 1977, plans went ahead to start a new A-level geology course. The Francis Scott Laboratory was well used, but with three and sometimes four groups, its two rooms plus a dark room and the geography laboratory nearby had become inadequate. In 1978, when the barn accommodation was complete, the top wooden building, which had been sleeping cubicles, was converted into a fourth laboratory, primarily for geology.

In the Brathay grounds, near Eagle Crag, there was a patch of boggy land which, after heavy rain, became a small lake, clearly reflecting the distant Langdale Pikes. It was a favourite spot of Francis Scott's in his latter years, and he was often taken there in his car to enjoy the view. The lake became a permanent feature of the landscape when Mortimer applied his African experience and a bulldozer to the creation of an earth dam to impound the small stream. The lake has appropriately become known as Mortimere, a name that has now found its way on to the Ordnance Survey map.

CENTRE FOR EXPLORATION AND FIELD STUDIES

In 1978, the BEG merged with the Field Study Centre to create the Brathay Centre for Exploration and Field Studies. This had been masterminded by Professor Bill Bishop, who had recently joined the governing body as chairman of the BEG committee. Sadly, he died before it was fully implemented. Michael Gee, a long-time associate of the BEG (and a nephew of Harvey Gee, the former general manager of the Provincial Insurance Co.), was appointed head of centre in 1979. The idea behind the merger was that since both groups were involved in discovery, a

closer association might encourage them to make better use of that common ground. The BEG, despite all its enterprise, probably needed a stronger sense of direction in its fieldwork: did it really make best use of its 'home' in the field centre? And did the Field Centre make best use of its exploration 'wing'? The distinguished people who made up the two committees now merged into one (thus reducing the administrative work) and, in the BEG, new life was given to a whole layer of volunteer specialists who planned the expeditions to various regions of the world.

Numbers attending the field centre continued to grow: 1980 was a record year (with 12,329 delegate days, almost the same number as the delegate days at the Hall). Despite this, the Field Centre was unable to make its proper contribution to central costs and this was a recurrent concern of the governors. In 1982 there was a further organisational reshuffle. After an extensive and democratic study of the options, the BEG decided on a separate (but not yet independent) existence. Under the influence of the Marsh report (see Theme 8), it was decided that 'the two-centre concept was no longer relevant' and that Brathay would now think in terms of 'activity areas'.

A separate centre committee now seemed irrelevant and was disbanded, with some members transferring to the main governing body. For the field study people, the new concept meant being redesignated as Environmental Studies, a name intended to embrace their current work plus their 'Environment without Frontiers' summer schools and related courses. It was an attempt to shift the emphasis away from geography/biology A-level, but it did not work. While many schools might pay lip service to a wider, environmentally-based curriculum, none were willing to support formal courses in this subject for their pupils. Nationally, schools were increasingly being judged by good examination results in conventional subjects. If Old Brathay was finding it a struggle to cover costs on a conventional course, what hope had it if it moved on to new ground? Scott's injunction to use 'freedom to experiment clear of any obligation to industry or any pressure from public authorities' no longer seemed to apply.

There was also the issue of teaching styles. After some soul-searching, many of the field centre staff expressed a wish to embrace a development training approach in their work, through which the students would be encouraged to accept responsibility for their own learning. The possibilities were exciting, but again there was a lack of schools prepared to support courses run in this manner. And no clients equalled no courses.

CENTRE FOR YOUTH LEARNING

With the arrival of the new principal David Richards, in 1983, Old Brathay, together with Eagle Crag, was renamed the Centre for Youth Learning, and from these two bases were run not only the field courses but also an expanding range of other courses, including many in response to the government's Manpower Services Commission Youth Training Schemes. There was a heavy demand for this kind of work and Brathay was well placed to give a lead: many saw it as just the kind of work for which Brathay was founded, and there was the expectation of such courses paying their way.

School field study courses continued in 1984 and 1985, but with rather lower levels of attendance. The income from these courses was not considered to be yielding a sufficient contribution to the central administration of Brathay, but price rises would only have meant a further decline in demand, so the work of the Field Study Centre was wound up in 1986. Schools and colleges were told that, in future all of Brathay's work would be in the realm of development training. Among the many letters of protest was one that commented:

I am led to understand that one of the aims of the Brathay Trust is to foster development of the individual, and respect for the environment. I would suggest that field studies do just this. The development they foster is mainly intellectual, but it is no less valuable than other aspects of development.

It was perhaps just as well that Mortimer did not survive to see the end of what had been his life for 15 years. He had died of a heart attack in August 1983. There had been a gathering in the barn in his honour at which many of his staff and colleagues reminisced about a brusque but loveable friend. To many in the education world, the centre's closure was like another death, and the protests were strong. But Brathay was having to live in the hard commercial world where idealism must be accompanied by a large cheque book. At the time of the closure, the commercial/altruistic debate (see Theme 8) seemed to pose a real dilemma. Even the Francis Scott Trust was unsympathetic towards the field centre. In an address to the assembled staff and governors in autumn 1983, its chairman said:

Field Studies did not form part of the charitable purpose of Brathay...It is self-evident that Brathay now lays great emphasis on management training, field studies and various other activities unconnected with Francis Scott's original conception of the courses.

THEME 5:
THE TURNING POINT, 1968–1975

This theme describes how the mainstream Brathay operation turned away from being one based almost entirely upon four-week 'self-discovery' courses. The needs of young people were changing and Brathay was responding to those needs. Brathay was also widening its client base, discovering that what worked well with young people could be adapted for others, both in the management field and for those with special social needs.

The core of the Brathay experience has remained virtually unchanged for over 40 years but steady evolution has taken place to reflect changing social mores. Communal prayers, for example, are no longer said daily. More is done to link the experience with the sponsor's objectives. Environmental issues, always a strong point, receive even more emphasis. Some of the modern approaches to training, such as neurolinguistic programming, have been built in. However, probably the most significant change has been the way in which the learning experience has been systematised.

When sponsors could afford four-week courses, it was possible to rely on a process akin to 'osmosis' to get the Brathay approach to learning absorbed. [In those days] the concrete experience of the Kolb learning cycle was the most systematically planned and designed of the four stages, and the remainder were sometimes left to chance – although the need to produce logs of one's experience helped in the reflective observation stage. However, when sponsors began pressing Brathay to shorten their courses, the only way of achieving the same outcome was to increase the effectiveness of the learning.

Dr Bertie Everard

If Outward Bound can claim much of the credit for advancing the practical development of adventurous activities, Brathay can claim an equally significant responsibility for developing a clearer understanding of the learning process.

Personal Growth Through Adventure, Hopkins and Putnam, 1993

Many would say that if something is going well you should leave it alone, but that has never been Brathay's way. The steady years of the 1960s were replaced by a re-ordering of the ways. Between 1960 and 1970 there was just one brochure, *Why Brathay? An Experiment in Self-discovery*. On the surface the only things that changed were the dates of the 10 courses a year, the person in charge and the fees. Although the fees had almost doubled over the previous decade, much of that increase could be put down to inflation. The old Holidays with Purpose tradition of keeping prices down so that sponsors or individuals should not be deterred continued with the Francis Scott Charitable Trust picking up the bill for between 35% and 50% of the actual running costs. High quality was more important to Scott than low costs, and money was always available to ensure that Brathay Hall and its furnishings were of a high standard. Besides running costs, the Trust's funds were also available whenever capital developments or improvements were needed. As a matter of policy, staff salaries were kept at a reasonable level for this type of work.

Numbers were well maintained at between 10,000 and 12,000 delegate days a year during the early 1960s, but people were beginning to make changes without fully realising why. By 1968 there was a feeling that the 'real needs' of young people were not being properly met, so Brathay sought ways to give sharper focus to the courses. The next few years were therefore to become a significant turning point in the history of Brathay.

To understand this period fully, it is necessary to look first at the background to the changes, which really had their roots in the early 1960s.

THE MEN IN CHARGE

The 1960s was a time of change in the leadership of Brathay, with five key people at the helm:

John Doogan, Mark Wolfson, Cameron Cochrane, Brian Ware and Denis Freeman. Doogan's later years were clouded by the onset of multiple sclerosis, and he had to retire in 1962. He moved to Glebe House, next door to Hawkshead Vicarage and into the devoted care of the vicar, Robert Lindsay, and his wife. During the few years left to him he was much called on by Brathay boys and by members of the Brathay Exploration Group (BEG). In an obituary in the *Westmorland Gazette* in January 1965, Francis Scott wrote of the:

...many hundreds of boys who came under his spell and felt that in Brathay they had a friend and an elder brother who was personally interested in each one of them.

David Price

During the short interregnum between Doogan's retirement and the arrival of Mark Wolfson, Alan Barrett, who had worked at Brathay as an instructor for several years, was the competent administrative officer. He carried a heavy load. David Price was the chief instructor. Both these men made significant contributions to Brathay, but shared leadership is never easy and for these two individuals there were difficulties as well as achievements.

Price was a greatly talented artist and sculptor, mountaineer, drama director and teacher. He was creative, interested and able at developing boys. In many ways, he epitomised both the skills and the ethos of Brathay at that time. Climbing a mountain and painting a picture, racing whalers on the lake and acting Dylan Thomas, were all of equal importance to him. Success in one activity could often instil confidence in another: the fat boy floundering up the mountain might shine in the play; the natural and overconfident sailor might be cut down to size in painting or sculpture. As chief instructor, Price set high standards in all these activities both for his staff and for those on the courses, but he did this in an informal and very individual manner, an approach that has remained a permanent strand of doing things the Brathay way.

Mark Wolfson

Mark Wolfson succeeded Doogan as warden in 1962 at the age of 28. Educated at Eton, Wolfson had done his National Service in the Navy, and read economics and geography at Cambridge, where he had been a successful oarsman, winning the Silver Goblets and other races at Henley, and taking the first British crew to Moscow since the 1917 revolution. After university, he worked in Canada as a teacher on a Red Indian reservation and then travelled through Africa before beginning a commercial career in London. He remembers:

I still wanted to do work that I could feel was more worthwhile. I was considering whether or not to go abroad again when a family friend and mentor, Hamish Blair-Cunynghame, suggested I could do such work here in the UK.

Blair-Cunynghame was a trustee of Brathay and suggested Wolfson apply for the vacant position of warden. Wolfson says, 'I applied, was offered and took the job, but not without many doubts. Would I be up to it, and was it really me?' He need not have worried. As it had for so many others, Brathay developed Wolfson and won his loyalty.

Although now the Member of Parliament for Sevenoaks, Kent, Wolfson has maintained his links with Brathay and is currently chairman of the trustees. Looking back over his years as warden he pays particular tribute to the dedicated and very able staff that he inherited and later recruited.

They really cared about their jobs, about how well our individual course members were doing, how well we could bring on those in difficulty, enable a team to work well, be successful and ensure that everyone left Brathay having experienced in some way a real feeling of achievement. That, for us, was the test of our own success or failure.

Mark Wolfson as warden, with Alan Barrett on his right and David Price on his left.

Mark Wolfson stayed for three and a half years, during which time numbers remained high. An innovation of his was 'Brathay Two', a follow-up course designed for those who wished to return for similar experiences the following year. One such course began at Brathay and then led on to climbing in Glencoe. Other courses were for those who wished to specialise in sailing, art or drama for one week during their annual holidays. In a way, it was a rebirth of Holidays with Purpose. Francis Scott had always wanted some opportunity of this kind to be provided on the campus, and this initiative anticipated the development of Tiny Wyke, the boathouse cottage in Pull Wyke Bay, as an 'Old Boys' Hut, sleeping 10, in 1979. By later standards, Brathay during Wolfson's time was relatively small and straightforward, and he saw his role as one of developing and expanding the facilities to provide something that was still almost unique. He was keen to develop the artistic side, and the appointment of Frank Singleton, a potter from Stoke-on-Trent, made it possible to offer pottery as an option on the art days. A kiln and a wheel were brought and installed in the old stable block art room. The fact that boys were there for a whole month was ideal since it allowed for the time gaps necessary for the various pottery processes. Some years later Singleton returned and is still on the Brathay staff.

Another development during this time was the junior courses. They began in 1965 and were the result of interest shown by Sir Percy Lord, chief education officer for Lancashire and a great Brathay supporter. They were 26 days long, for boys aged 14–16 years, and, in effect, were simply a milder version of the standard four-week course. In one form or another the junior courses continued for the following 13 years and presaged the development, some 30 years later, of the current personal and social education work.

Cameron Cochrane

Wolfson left Brathay in 1966 to become head of the Youth Services of the Industrial Society. His successor as warden was A. J. Cameron Cochrane who had been an English teacher at St Edward's School, Oxford. Cochrane was a family man with two young children and it was a delight to see Brathay Knott, the stylish wooden Colt house, fully occupied for the first time. The house had been built for Doogan, his wife and teenage son, but was not completed until the winter of 1954/55, just as his wife died and he was taking over as warden.

Restructuring of Brathay under Ware

Cochrane arrived in 1966 just as other important developments were occurring that eventually led to a complete restructuring of Brathay and the foundation of the Field Study Centre (see Theme 4). These changes also heralded the return, in a larger role, of someone who had been involved in Brathay from its earliest days. Ware came to Brathay with a dual responsibility. Initially, he was tasked with setting up the Field Study Centre but he was also to be the first director of Brathay, responsible for the general co-ordination of all Brathay's activities.

After his time on the Brathay staff in the days of Holidays with Purpose, Ware taught at Hertford Grammar School. He moved to Cambridgeshire as further education tutor at Impington Village College in 1949, and in 1953 he went to Uppingham School to teach geography, coach athletics and hockey, and be housemaster, and act as a link with the Uppingham/Corby Boys' Club (whose members had been early supporters of Holidays with Purpose). At all these places he formed links with Brathay, and he maintained personal contact by remaining as honorary secretary of the BEG.

Developments under Cochrane

During the latter part of the 1960s, Cochrane steered the Hall courses along a path that combined the traditional elements that had been so successful over the years with a few changes of direction to build for the future. These changes were defined in an addition to the 1968 brochure.

The course now lasts 26 days and the programme includes pottery, orienteering, canoeing and community service. There has also been an increasing emphasis in the discussion group sessions on the relationship of the Brathay activities to the world of work – an attempt to be more precise about the service we provide, principally for young men from industry and commerce but also for schoolboys, Borstal boys, boys on probation, police cadets and boys from overseas.

About this time there was a small but significant change in staff titles. Staff at the Field Study Centre were called tutors. To call the Hall staff 'instructors' seemed to denigrate their role, so they too henceforth became known as tutors. Another change, in 1969, was that the four-week course in May was the first to include girls.

THE INDUSTRIAL SOCIETY AND ITS LINKS WITH BRATHAY

The Industrial Society was founded in 1918 as the Industrial Welfare Society 'to help those who lead in industry and the trade unions to see the way forward to the greater involvement of people's gifts at work'. It mainly provides training courses and conferences for all levels and aspects of management. With regard to young people in the 1960s, the society felt that too many talents and abilities were underused and that, as a result, individuals were increasingly frustrated by dull work in vast organisations. The society saw its role not in job skills training or further education but in involvement, helping young people to develop greater commitment to their work.

One early enterprise that the society helped to set up was the Duke of York's Camps, an enterprise dear to Scott's heart.

Brathay had strong links with the society, the earliest being that John Marsh, the society's director from 1949 to 1961, was a former member of the Brathay Hall management committee. The director of the Industrial Society in 1968 was John Garnett, who had formerly worked for ICI, which was a substantial supporter of Brathay in its first 25 years, and, from 1966, the head of the society's youth services department was Wolfson.

In 1969, Brathay and the Industrial Society together devised a totally new course. Called Responsibility at Work, it was aimed at young men aged 18–21 years to help them 'relate the experience of leadership, responsibility and teamwork on the mountains, and of creative opportunity, to greater effectiveness at work'. The course lasted 14 days, included all the normal

Cameron Cochrane, seated centre, with a typical four week course, 1966.

Brathay activities except sailing, and was run jointly by staff from Brathay and from the Industrial Society.

The first Responsibility at Work course was held in January 1969 with 28 young apprentices. In 1970 there were four such courses plus an additional eight-day course called Preparing for Leadership. This was for people aged from 18 years to their early 20s who were moving for the first time into positions where they would have responsibility for other people. Both these courses became a regular part of the annual programme.

Another link between Brathay and the Industrial Society came through its associate director, Dr (later Professor) John Adair. Adair brought a new way of thinking about training based on what he called Action-Centred Leadership (ACL), which he had introduced to the Royal Military Academy, Sandhurst, in 1964 while he was senior lecturer and training adviser there. In essence, Adair's approach involved thinking about three needs: defining the job or *task*, building up the *team*, and satisfying the *individual*. This concept is often expressed as three overlapping circles (see illustration). These ideas were soon being widely promoted by the Industrial Society to firms all over the country.

At Ware's invitation, Adair visited Brathay in 1970 so that his ideas could be incorporated into the leadership courses. Cochrane had been succeeded as warden by Denis Freeman, another Uppingham master but one with a military background. Such qualities must have helped in the acceptance of the new ideas that had been such a success at Sandhurst.

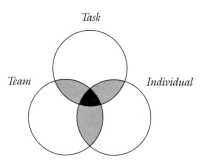

John Adair.

BACKGROUND TO THE CHANGES

Brathay had been aware for a while of the deficiencies in its regular programme of four-week courses, particularly the routine way in which many firms sent young people on courses without any strong reasons for doing so other than feeling that it was a 'good thing'. At the same time, many companies were beginning to examine their reasons for sending people, and the decline in numbers attending four-week courses indicated that some were voting with their feet. Four weeks, they felt, was too long a time to spend away from the workplace and the cost was too high.

One company that looked closely at the four-week courses and assessed their value was British Leyland. The following comments were gathered by Geoffrey Holroyde, British Leylands's head of apprentice training, when he attended one of the four-week courses at Brathay in 1971. Holroyde later became chairman of the Brathay governing body.

1. *The course was very strenuous, certainly not a holiday, but it gave a chance to look at the work scene from a distance.*
2. *They learnt to understand other people. They had gained confidence in their ability to get on with others, and deal with conflict. This would help them to supervise.*
3. *They had learnt to overcome problems, not to duck them or rush for help. They had appreciated that they had the ability to deal with far tougher situations than they had previously believed.*
4. *Getting cross with people doesn't work, and doesn't improve group results. You have to put up with others' weaknesses in order to use their strengths.*
5. *They are better disciplined personally, from inside, and realise the need to order their own lives and work.*
6. *They recognise the need to plan ahead, to recognise problems, to organise oneself, to use time effectively, not to waste other people's time.*
7. *They had learnt to communicate, to express opinions, to listen. The drama had given them confidence to talk in groups and express their views, whereas previously they might have remained passive or silent.*
8. *The art and the pottery had taught them patience.*
9. *They had developed ideas about how to use their leisure time most constructively.*
10. *They felt able to face up to life and its difficulties, and to deal with them.*
11. *They felt this experience would make them better employees: more confident, determined to succeed, more co-operative, more responsible.*
12. *They felt that, for similar reasons, they would be better citizens.*
13. *They were disappointed that so few of their colleagues had similar chances.*
14. *They could not understand why this kind of experience was not a compulsory part of education and training, and why they had not been developed along these lines before. There is a potential lying dormant in too many people.*
15. *They felt that a month at Brathay did more for them than a year at the 'tech'.*

Such positive feedback was echoed in *The Challenge of Outward Bound* (D. Fletcher, 1971), which described the extent and benefits of courses run by the highly successful Outward Bound Trust.

However, adventurous training received criticism three years later from *The Character Training Industry* (Roberts, White and Parker), which set out to examine why people were sent on outdoor courses. Both Brathay and Outward Bound had become victims of their own success in that, while many firms felt the courses were a good thing, they had no clear understanding of what the benefits might be. If there were ways of giving a sharper focus to the work and of helping firms to understand the real purpose of the courses, now was the time. In Brathay's case this refocusing had already begun with the introduction of the Responsibility at Work course, although the traditional four-week course remained the backbone. To make a serious change in direction it was necessary to have much more evidence of what the needs of young people and industry really were.

The Whitfield report

It was consequently decided to commission research into the effectiveness of the traditional four-week courses, and Ware approached the Department of Behaviour in Organisations at Lancaster University for assistance. It was decided to conduct a pilot study to examine the aspirations, expectations and post-course assessment of course members, their sponsoring organisations, and the staff involved. The survey was carried out by Peter Whitfield, an RAF Squadron Leader, who obtained responses from some 74 companies who had used Brathay over the previous 22 years. The results, published in summary in the June 1974 edition of *Industrial and Commercial Training*, confirmed that the time was ripe for change.

Whitfield found that 'the term "Outward Bound" is widely used by firms as a generic title for all courses and that, at the supervisor/trainee interface there is little or no knowledge of the differing aims, content or even location of the many courses on offer'. (Outward Bound is, of course, the brand name of the Outward Bound Trust).

Whitfield also found:

Selection procedures are very varied...Many large firms...allocate numbers of vacancies to regional offices and call for nominations. Some simply advertise on notice boards and leave the initiative to the trainee. In very few organisations was there any real evidence of matching individually identified training needs with the specific course content of a particular centre.

As for the benefits of going on a course, he said:

There is a widespread feeling expressed by training officers of 'intangible but real benefits' but that the individual benefits more than the company.

Firms seemed philosophical about this, as they were about the whole matter of the benefit is to them from apprentice training. Apprentices tended to leave their firms in large numbers at the end of their training, but firms felt that in the long run there might be some benefit from all their investment. Even so, 'very few of the sponsor firms mentioned expectations of enhanced commitment or company loyalty to follow from attendance at courses, and not one mentioned either expecting or observing any willingness to work harder'. In fairness, there was no such claim in Brathay's literature at the time.

Whitfield found there to be a general lack of debriefing or follow-up on the experience of the courses, and concluded that, as a result, 'much of the potential value of the course is lost'. As for the students' view of the benefits of the course, Whitfield found that 60% were positive, 19% negative, and the rest were neutral.

A four-week course evaluation

Whitfield made his own assessment of a Brathay course by attending and observing 'Rydal Dormitory Group' throughout their four weeks.

The emphasis in the early phase was on instruction but only insofar as it hastened the point at which the learning process could become self-sustaining. The eventual aim was to give the students a learning experience in the effective use of individual and group resources so that, in the final week, each group was able to depart on a full three-day trekking expedition unaccompanied by any staff, carrying all necessary camping kit, food and spares and to report back to the group tutor with a full account of the events, problems and solutions they experienced.

Much in evidence in all the activities over the four weeks was the gradual withdrawal of the tutor from the straight teaching role to that of a nominal presence concerned with safety or supervision but primarily acting as a catalyst in small group interaction. With a skilful tutor – in this case teacher-trained and very experienced in military and expedition life – it was soon evident that the task was not to teach climbing, pottery, rowing, etc. but that these were vehicles to generate and illustrate the processes of group dynamics. The relationships between the various group tasks and the students' more workaday world were constantly being highlighted. An important part of the Brathay philosophy is that, apart from one orienteering event and an end-of-course regatta, there is no attempt to generate competitiveness; the stress was on team achievement using the team's resources and expertise, experience, personality and motivation to achieve group tasks.

In conclusion, Whitfield said:

What does emerge with clarity...is that the properly briefed and motivated student who is also given follow-up support and interest by his sponsor derives real benefit.

The final part of Whitfield's comment is significant. Although it states what many feel is obvious, this was the first time that anyone had established, by direct observation, that there was benefit to be gained from a course.

The outcomes of the report

Despite its high praise for the Brathay approach, the Whitfield report was, in effect, an obituary for the four-week courses, and bookings for them fell steadily. In its bones the Brathay management was already aware that industry, despite its muddle-headedness about character training courses (as many still described them), was ready for something more sharply focused. In its response to Whitfield's report in the same issue of *Industrial and Commercial Training*, Brathay made two main points.

1. The need to improve links with sponsors: 'Re-examining Brathay's objectives and strengths, applying lessons learned from student/sponsor expectations and feedback as well as from findings in the behavioural sciences, developing new patterns of course content to meet specific needs, and establishing more solidly-based sponsor/Brathay relationships'.
2. Diversification of courses based on: 'the close identification of Brathay with industry/commerce and its needs, and the recognition, largely as a result of close association with the Industrial Society, that Brathay had an environment and facilities well fitted to bringing alive behavioural science teaching in practical learning situations. On the one hand, sponsors were looking for a more intensive work-related course which would enable potential key staff to live through and learn from real human relations situations. At the same time, John Adair's Action-Centred Leadership/Group Needs framework, with its proved practical value, could ideally be conveyed in the action-centred context of Brathay Hall'.

MAKING THE CHANGES

Researching the future

Brathay was now moving strongly towards a new pattern of working: shorter and more sharply focused courses for young people (and not only young workers) plus more specialised courses for those (often older people) who were destined for leadership and management. Once again, as in junior work, Brathay decided to check reaction to its innovations with research.

Two years after producing the first report, Whitfield was invited back in 1975 to study one of the 15-day Preparing for Leadership courses. He found that, although still feeling its way, Brathay was developing a new pattern in management work. His preliminary conclusions gave a very clear picture of how and why Brathay turned towards a new dual approach, covering both young people and management. He showed that the early 1970s were not only a turning point, but a branching of the ways. Prophetically, he pointed out that diversity could cause problems in deciding who Brathay's main customers were. Whitfield wrote:

All my conversations with staff at Brathay seemed to indicate that the Hall stands at an important decision point in history. Indeed there was some feeling in certain quarters that it may already have drifted beyond the decision point and that trends were perhaps being established which were not the result of a full analysis of the situation, but which might nevertheless prove irreversible. That decision is of course concerned with the product mix of the organisation. There is a real need to establish clearly what business the Hall is in and then harness the estate's resources and the wholehearted commitment of the staff to excel in that business.

The Hall's origins lay in providing unique experiences of challenging tasks in a rural environment to the relatively deprived young people of post-war urban Britain. The standard course provided a splendid contribution to this aim for a quarter of a century. However, the social and economic environment from which the Hall drew its customers has undergone considerable change and it is evident that, in an inflationary age, demand for this product has declined. Or it might be that the demand is still there but that the source of funds has shifted. The industrial sponsor appears to be demanding some more tangible return on his investment and seems more prepared to support courses which are more closely aligned with his training needs. The sponsorship for the 'urban deprived', who still exist in large numbers, may now be from the welfare agencies, social services, charitable institutions or other non-profit-seeking bodies.

The question which Brathay must ask itself, and find a definite answer to, is whether its mission still lies in the provision of valuable personal development training on a broad front for the widest possible student population, or whether to move into the area of specific training to a selected (and perhaps elitist) student body. It may be felt that the Hall can fulfil both roles, but, from my observations of the two courses I have now seen, I think it is unlikely that a staff could be recruited which would be able to throw itself wholeheartedly into both types of course since the whole ethos is so different.

If the standard (four-week) course becomes a casualty in this decision-making process – and I stress that I do not think this in any way to be a foregone conclusion – then the staff must be reconciled to the fact that their role is now more that of a professional trainer than a broad educationalist. Their credibility, both with students and their sponsor organisations, will depend on their commitment to, and professional expertise in, leadership training. It would, therefore, be essential that they should have proper training themselves in the theory and practice of ACL (action-centred leadership) or whatever other approach may be developed, and that the fullest possible use is made of the range of activities available to Brathay students to promote understanding and practice in the skills of leadership.

The outcomes

Typically, Brathay was not slow to react to these observations. In fact many changes had already begun to take place in advance of the publication of the second Whitfield report. The post-Whitfield position, in 1975, is summarised below.

1. Three 25-day standard courses. One mixed. Age 17–21. The last year of such courses.
2. Four 14-day junior courses. Age 14–16. (Comprising one large course at the Hall plus three courses of 24 at the BEG huts.)
3. Four 15-day Responsibility at Work courses for apprentices. Age 18–22.
4. Three 10-day Leadership for Managers courses (with the Industrial Society). Age under 30.
5. Two nine-day Managers in Action courses (with the Industrial Society). Age up to 50.
6. One seven-day follow-up course – to continue special interests.
7. Four 14-day special company courses (ICI, Post Office, John Lewis).
8. Several 10-day Trident courses (see Theme 6). Age 14–16. Usually at the BEG huts.
9. One eight-day mountain leadership course.
10. Thirty-four seven-day field study courses (yielding 10,444 delegate days), approximately 60% schools, 30% colleges.
11. Twenty Exploration Group expeditions (yielding 5806 delegate days), 363 participants.

The total estimated 1975 delegate days for Brathay as a whole was 25,450.

The Acland report

Some years after it had fully adopted the 'new style' courses, John Acland, an independent researcher, was appointed to do a sixth-month study of training methods, mainly with a view to the production of a strategy for the wider promotion of Brathay work under the Brathay Extension Service (see Theme 8). What follows is an extract from a case study in his report.

It is the fifth day of the course. The members are all in their early 20s and come from a well established retailing company in which they have all recently achieved positions of responsibility. Morale is already high, for the group has performed all its tasks competently and built up plenty of team spirit. A problem lurks, however, in the shape of Bill. He emerges in the very first hour of the course as a brash extrovert, apparently highly satisfied with his own constantly paraded sense of humour.

The morning session is in the creative workshop and one of the group's tasks, with Bill appointed as leader, is to make a montage of their drawings. The organisation is so inept that soon every course member is idle except for Bill himself. He is drawing jokey captions. This is too much for Jenny who makes a brief explosive outburst before retreating to the sidelines, simmering gently.

After lunch, the group is driven off to a remote mountain hut, sparsely equipped with bunk beds, tables and benches. In the afternoon they go caving in some disused copper mines, abseiling from one level to another in the dark.

After clearing up the supper, they sit in candlelight around a glowing wood stove. The conversation is drifting gently around various aspects of the course when suddenly, unprompted, Jenny rounds on Bill and vehemently expresses her anger both over the montage and over his exasperating sense of humour. The following three hours see a discussion of great intensity involving every member of the group. At first the accent is on what Bill calls his character assasination. For parts of this he is so obviously upset that he withdraws into the shadows. Gradually the group switches from an accusatory tone to a questioning one and he reveals that he is having considerable problems at work. Despite his recent promotion, he finds it hard to wield authority, largely because his attitude ensures that he can never be anything but 'one of the boys'. Finally, the group reveals the many ways in which it appreciates him and it makes a whole host of suggestions for him to modify his behaviour in a way which will make the most of his good points.

It is hard to describe the emotional intensity of that evening. Certainly it was enough to affect one physically; to make the skin tingle and the stomach tighten. Certainly it is not enough to describe it in careful terms like 'group cohesion' or 'mutual support'. At least one observer saw it as an outpouring of love. However you describe it, it was enough to change Bill's attitude radically for the rest of the course and he took away written plans for making similar changes at work. It was also enough to usher in a new dimension to the group's later discussions; a dimension which allowed many deeply controversial issues to be exposed and to be sensitively explored.

Conclusion

By the mid-1970s, new theories – such as the Kolb cycle, and action-centred leadership – were being regularly used at Brathay to good effect. As a tribute to the man who had been at the helm throughout this crucial period, Ware received an OBE in the Queen's Birthday Honours of 1972.

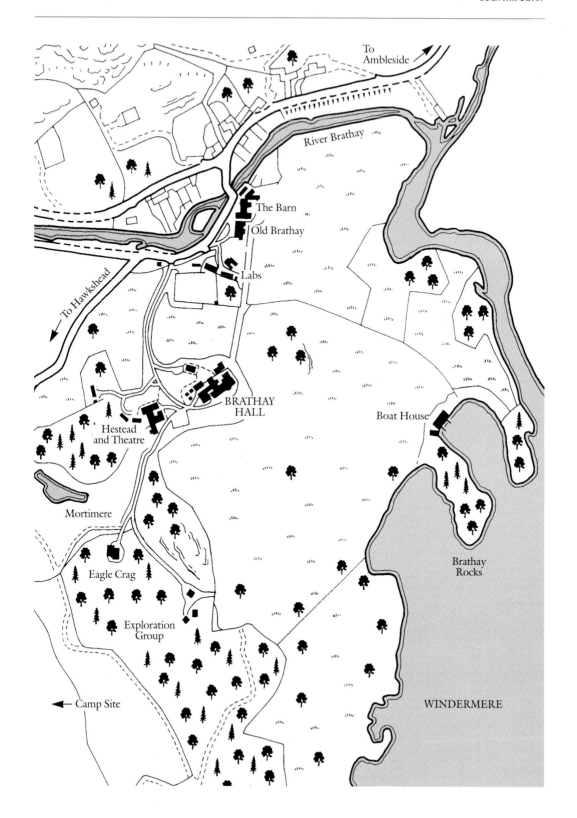

To
Ambleside

River Brathay

The Barn

Old Brathay

To Hawkshead

Labs

BRATHAY
HALL

Boat House

Hestead
and Theatre

Mortimere

Eagle Crag

Brathay
Rocks

Exploration
Group

Camp Site

WINDERMERE

THEME 6:
DEVELOPMENTS IN YOUTH WORK

Brathay has always sought to help young people with particular needs, following the example of its founder, who did much work with the disadvantaged before founding Brathay (see Theme 1). Even when the main and very absorbing work of the four-week courses began, there was still room for a few special events. Former staff member George Pettingale brought up the boys from his special school in Oxfordshire, and Brian Ware arranged residential courses for the employees from Chivers jam factory.

THE CHIVERS GIRLS' COURSES (1950s)

Chivers' main factory was in Histon, a village adjoining Impington in Cambridgeshire. Impington was well known in the education world as the home of one of the first village colleges, founded in Cambridgeshire to provide not just a school but a wide range of educational and social opportunities for the local community. To this end, their premises included a library, an adult wing and a large community hall. The person in charge was called a warden (who was also head of the school) and the staff included a tutor for further and adult education. Ware was such a tutor at Impington, and his responsibilities included organising the tuition programme of the Day Continuation School run by Chivers. The company released its young employees for half a day each week for a programme of general education. Employers were not obliged to offer such opportunities and it was only the more enlightened, such as Cadburys, Chivers or ICI that did so. In the case of Chivers, the great majority of those attending were girls since most of the boys were apprentices and therefore attended the work-orientated courses at the local technical college on their half day.

The proposed County College pattern had envisaged a short residential experience. Although this was never implemented, Chivers supported Ware in arranging for a group of girls to spend a week at Brathay. The girls came up each summer during the early 1950s, in the pause between two boys' courses, and spent a week taking part in the usual range of activities of that time: fell-walking, boating, and sessions in the art room. They slept in the dormitories and were probably the first female outdoor education course ever to be held in a national residential centre.

THE 1955 OXFORDSHIRE SCHOOLBOY COURSES

Boys who think that being selected for a Brathay Oxford means an easy time or a holiday from school are mistaken. The course toughens them both physically and mentally. On this course, for instance, we have done surveying in hot weather and in the rain. We lived up in the mountains for a week. At Brathay we are looked after extremely well. The food is excellent and the medical care efficient. I have only one criticism – we don't get enough free time! But I wouldn't have missed the opportunity of coming here for the world.

So wrote a 14-year-old boy who took part in another of Brathay's pioneering ventures. It began in 1955 in association with Oxfordshire Education Authority in the person of its director of education, A.R. Chorlton. The authority's senior officer, R.C.E. Naish, had expressed interest in developing residential courses for secondary modern schoolboys in their last (fourth) year of secondary education, at that time something quite new. Few youngsters went on school trips lasting more than a day and to many the idea of going away from home, without parents, for six weeks was unthinkable. However, to Francis Scott, the idea, or at least the aspiration, was already there. We have seen how he supported the early boys clubs' residentials, and in the 1950s he also supported camps of young workers from the TLF group of Sunderland shipyards, which had a permanent hut in the Brathay fields. Of the 14- and 15-year-olds still at school, Scott wrote:

Recent developments, particularly in the raising of the school leaving age, have suggested that there is very real scope to extend this [residential] opportunity not only to those already in industry, but to those in the last year or two of school life.

As a result of the Oxfordshire approach, a series of six-week courses was planned by Brathay staff in collaboration with staff from Oxfordshire. The courses were based on the well tried formula for the four-week courses but also included a whole range of schoolwork, giving an outdoor element to many of the normal subjects. They had the run of the Brathay facilities: the boats, the art room, the tents and mountain equipment, and the expertise of the Brathay staff. The courses were based at Old Brathay which was converted for youth use for the first time. Before then it had been in fitful use as a conference centre or a base for the odd Central Council of Physical Recreation teachers' course or British Council foreign students' residential. The main rooms became simple dormitories so that they could accommodate 24 boys in three groups of eight. Such was Oxfordshire's faith in the scheme that it was prepared to go for four six-week courses a year (two in the summer term and one each in spring and autumn) with a guaranteed 24 boys and two staff on each course. The best gauge of the pupils' reactions to the courses are their own reports, extracts from which follow.

Our stamina and fitness have vastly improved...the weather has been fine but the mountain work extremely testing and strenuous, but also we can now take a three-mile run-and-walk in boots almost in our stride.

We could throw in a stone [in a cave] and count the seconds until it reached the bottom. Not a little disturbed, we soon came out. We went up to Brathay Hall to hear a lecture on mountain rescue by Dr Madge. His visual aids were: one bloodhound, one blood-stained sixpence and one piece of human skull. Preparations were under way for the end-of-course concert. After having seen the show put on by the lads from industry at the Hall, we decided to organise ourselves...Royston Payne is full of sinister ideas. Eddie Tait has turned dramatic actor. Paul Austin is to be the debonair compère.

As the sun sinketh in the west,
And our eyelids close to rest,
Then do we see the true glory of God.
In each ripple on each tarn,
In each shadow on each mount;
And all our blessings without count,
Show themselves before our weary eyes...
He hath shown us all,
At the coming of nightfall.

The last account is from the *Assistant Masters' Association Journal* and was written by J. Eggeleston:

Boys were selected for several reasons – because they were suited to an adventurous life, or they were candidates for the Duke of Edinburgh's Award, or for therapeutic reasons. By the middle of the course, leaders have emerged – often from the least likely source. These are the boys who will be running their own expeditions and schoolwork projects by the end of the course...Progress is certainly evident – mental and physical. An unmistakable sense of purpose and self-awareness develops in most boys – they seem not only mature but more balanced – certainly they are often more pleasant and likeable human beings.

The Oxfordshire courses continued for four years, by which time the Oxfordshire staff were clearly able to run their own show. So they moved to the YMCA centre at Patterdale Hall where they continued successfully for many years.

It is difficult for those close to Brathay to make an objective assessment of the long-term effects of the Oxfordshire courses. There is no doubt that those who attended benefited greatly. In a

simple way the participants were getting a great many of the benefits of a boarding school whose virtues were advocated in the Fleming report of 1944 (on the possible integration of public schools into the state education system). That Oxfordshire was prepared to invest so much money into the scheme is testament to its view of its worth. Even at Scott-subsidised Brathay, the expense of sending 96 boys a year away from home for six weeks was considerable. While no other counties were prepared to run residentials for ordinary lads on this scale, the national records over the following decades show that these were the years when many counties set up their own residential centres for a whole range of purposes. The ones that flourished were those that had some speciality such as mountain walking, sailing/canoeing, or field studies. The concept of a general course of the Brathay/Oxfordshire type never really caught on, and perhaps this was because most of those promoting the courses (unlike Oxfordshire's director of education) were specialists who simply wanted to promote their field. The whole art of running general courses got lost, as was realised when the government offered Manpower Services Commission money for residential experiences incorporated into training schemes for the unemployed in the 1970s, and when the TVEI (Technical and Vocational Education Initiative, see later) schemes were introduced in the 1980s. Handbooks (some Brathay-inspired) had to be produced to help the new generation of providers, and the Development Training Advisory Group (DTAG) found it necessary to offer training courses for teachers on 'Making the Most of a Residential' for the TVEI people.

It is only now, in the mid-1990s, with schools being required to give prominence to Personal and Social Education (PSE), that we are again seeing the rebirth of the idea of an all-round residential experience. And, typically, Brathay is active in this field too. (There is a picture of Oxfordshire boys and their teacher on page 26.)

CAMPING AT BRATHAY

For those whose Brathay experience is mostly between four walls it is easy to forget that Scott's vision of the place had always included camping. The original National Association of Boys' Clubs (NABC) experiences were largely based on camping and, as already mentioned, the Sunderland shipbuilding group TLF had a permanent base in the grounds for its annual summer camp. Few places can be more picturesque than the arms of headland by the boathouse, a venue for Brathay Exploration Group (BEG) practice camps or returning old boys. A big Scout Jamboree was held at Brathay one year in the early 1960s, and not long afterwards a well appointed campsite, administered by the Scouts but open to all, was established at the west end of the estate. This site is now the far point in the orienteering route for those on the Hall's management course, and a group leader of some youngsters staying on the campsite recalls that his boys got so used to seeing these keen men racing past their tents with their clipboards and compasses through the night, that if they looked lost the boys would offer: 'Give us a quid and I'll tell you where the checkpoint is!'.

THE TRIDENT TRUST COURSES

The Trident Trust was founded in 1970 as an independent educational charity (funded by industry and the Dulverton Trust) designed to help young people in the transition from school to working life. The three 'prongs' of the Trident programme were: work experience, voluntary community service, and personal development. This last aim was to be achieved in the main through a residential outdoor course for which Brathay was ideally suited. The age group of people nominated was 14–16 years, exactly that of the junior courses from Lancashire just coming to an end at that time because of education authority budget cuts. Brathay staff were therefore well able to cope with this new challenge, and in close co-operation with Bob Newman, the Trident co-ordinator, from 1973 several Trident courses were organised each year, becoming a significant part of Brathay's annual programme. Using Brathay's best development training practice, many interesting ideas and approaches were explored in fostering all-round personal and social development. Although Trident courses were run in many places, Brathay was one of the most important centres used as far as the Trident organisers were concerned.

Young people came from schools in all parts of the country, nominated by regional Trident co-ordinators who were managers seconded by industrial and commercial companies. The groups of 10 to 20 youngsters were usually based in the BEG huts during term-time when the BEG was not using them. Later, the courses were held at the new Eagle Crag centre (see later). For a time, young people were also nominated for UK expeditions with the BEG. By 1984, there were five Trident courses a year, and by 1987 Trident accounted for 6% of Brathay's total clientele, according to the annual report. In 1988 Trident 'delegate days' amounted to 688 (15%) out of a total of 4706 for youth work.

INTERMEDIATE TREATMENT

The initials IT are generally understood to mean information technology in current parlance. But at Brathay in the 1970s they stood for a style of youth work then becoming important that entailed outdoor work with young people who had been in trouble. Intermediate treatment (IT) came into being as a result of the Children and Young Persons Act, 1969, and formed an essential part of the policies for dealing with juvenile offenders. IT schemes aimed to reduce delinquency by involving young people in constructive activities, offering them opportunities for achievement, improving their social skills and bringing them into contact with mature adults who could exercise a positive influence on them and provide counselling, both individual and in groups. While most IT facilities were provided by local authorities' social services departments, voluntary organisations also played an important part and pioneered much innovatory practice. It is here that Brathay made a significant contribution, notably in developing programmes to include short residential experiences.

Brathay had always been concerned with making a useful contribution to the treatment of 'problem kids'. For some 20 years up to 12 boys from Borstal establishments were sponsored each year by the Home Office to attend normal Brathay courses. The boys were usually willing to acknowledge their Borstal connection during the course introductions and were accepted like everyone else. They generally thrived in the friendly, informal and supportive atmosphere of Brathay, and post-course contacts revealed many success stories among those who had made good use of this special opportunity. There was rather less success, however, with four gang leaders from the then notorious Easterhouse estate in Glasgow who were all sponsored on the same 26-day course. After a few days, their anxiety about who might be replacing them as gang leaders was too much, and they had to be sent home!

Brathay's staff were keen to find other specific ways of contributing constructively to the increasing problems of young people with particular difficulties, and Ware remembers this view being strongly articulated at a staff meeting in 1975. At a time of critical change at Brathay, there was a feeling that the demands of industry were growing at the expense of the needs of less advantaged young people. The message from the staff was clear: Brathay should identify an area of work with disadvantaged youth where their special skills and experience might contribute something of value. A suitable opportunity was soon found.

Joint scheme with St Helens social services

At Peter Scott's suggestion, Ware had been developing contacts with the Dartington Hall Trust. A visit by Spencer Millham of the Dartington Social Services Unit led to an introduction to the St Helens social services in Merseyside. This department was seeking new ways to divert young people from crime and so lessen the dependence on residential or custodial care. Six small groups had been formed of children 'at risk', meeting weekly with two or three social workers, and now the department was looking to build some short-term residential experience into the scheme.

A meeting was therefore arranged at Brathay in which a group of social workers outlined the problems, and Brathay tutors demonstrated the centre's expertise and resources. The result was a joint IT venture, with roots firmly in the child's own community, but with carefully integrated residential experiences at Brathay. Each group of about 10 children plus their social workers was to come to Brathay for three weekends and a five-day period (i.e. a total of 11 days) in each year. Brathay agreed to allocate a member of staff to work closely with each group's social workers in planning and leading activities at Brathay, and to visit the group regularly in St Helens. Accommodation was provided in the basic 'mountain hut' bunk rooms of the BEG quarters on a self-catering basis.

The whole project and its special character ultimately depended on the Brathay tutor. The children came with high expectations: hills, woods, lake, an exciting ropes course, fun, danger, new experiences, and the creative workshop. Learning to live and work together effectively as members of a small group was fundamental to the project and it was the tutor who had to select and blend the appropriate ingredients from the wide range of Brathay activities. It was not easy.

Chris Moore, one of the first Brathay tutors to be involved, wrote:

Traditionally, people come to Brathay to adjust. We have varied programmes to suit particular needs, but there is always the basic form, structure, procedure, which is Brathay. It is planned and it works. We put ourselves in the attacking position and issue the challenges...With the St Helens boys, we are suddenly off our guard, on the defensive. They do the attacking, they are offering the challenges – to us – to society. 'Give us what we need, give us our due, or we will fight you.' At no time in my three years at Brathay were greater demands made on me than during the St Helens weekends.

The scheme got under way in 1976, with 21 group visits involving a total of 58 children together with usually two or three social workers for each group. When the year's work was reviewed, it was noted that only eight of the children had since been taken into residential care. In 1978 there were 28 group visits with some 70 children taking part. On the Brathay side, David England, Richard LeMare and then Jim and Janet Dobson took charge of this work, showing imagination and great dedication.

The new approach to tackling the problems of juvenile delinquency pioneered by Brathay and the St Helens social services gave rise to widespread interest. A weekend conference to demonstrate the main elements of the scheme was held at Brathay in May 1977. Eighteen social services departments from the north of England were represented, and six expressed interest in starting similar schemes in conjunction with Brathay when additional accommodation became available.

Lancaster University research project

In 1979, the Centre of Youth, Crime and Community at Lancaster University obtained a major grant from the Department of Health and Social Security to carry out an in-depth study of the St Helens scheme over a year. The project was directed by Dr David Thorpe and involved three experienced participant observers, each attached to two of the St Helens groups. Outdoor pursuits had got a bad name because of too close an association with IT in the past, as a result of which this kind of activity was denied any place at all in the programmes for youth at risk by some authorities. One of the researchers, David Smith had himself been openly critical of the use of outdoor education in intermediate treatment. However, after a year's close association with Brathay's well refined approach to personal and social development, he felt able to report favourably on the scheme (in the first Francis C. Scott Memorial Lecture at the Policy Studies Institute in 1982). He said:

Many juveniles...have reported feeling that outdoor activities were a form of punishment...If you look through the literature you will rarely find a coherent, convincing account of just what the values of outdoor education are meant to be.

Smith felt that there was a risk in Brathay thinking that what it did so well with managers and young workers could easily be transposed to juvenile offenders. However, he then went on to say:

Periods spent at Brathay have remained uniquely valued experiences in the collective life of intermediate treatment groups and in the memories of the individual offenders in them...They have also provided social workers with a direct knowledge of the characteristics of offenders in their charge which they could probably not have acquired in any other setting. Social workers take risks when they share testing experiences with juvenile offenders: risks with their own authority and status, and the risk of finding out things about their clients which it would be more comfortable not to know. Extremes emerge in an unfamiliar and demanding environment which remain safely hidden in everyday contexts – extremes of destructiveness, anger or despair, as well as surprising capacities and talents...Tense but authentic emotional relationships can develop in a setting like Brathay. Something of the reality of a juvenile's experience of himself may emerge there which could remain hidden forever in the more polite and comfortable settings of the office or family home. This kind of explosive and undeniable revelation is not easy for either the worker or the juvenile, and it requires skill in its handling. But it does make possible a more open and potentially more honest level of communication in the future.

THE EAGLE CRAG CENTRE

By 1979 it was clear that purpose-built accommodation would be needed if the scope of Brathay's involvement in IT was to develop. The existing arrangements to use spare capacity at the BEG huts limited the project to five IT groups, catering for some 60 children annually. A new unit to accommodate up to 12 children would increase the annual capacity to 20 groups and 250 children annually. The Brathay trustees, encouraged by the success of the pilot scheme with St Helens and the growing interest of other local authorities, decided to plan a new centre.

Brathay's architect, Robert Gilchrist, entered fully into the spirit and purpose of the new enterprise. Meetings with tutors and social workers ensured that full use was made of their ideas and of the valuable experience of the previous four years. Experience showed that the children responded well to the 'log cabin/mountain hut' atmosphere where, as a 'house group', they would be involved in all the household tasks of cooking, washing up, cleaning and maintenance. Roger Greenaway, a tutor at Eagle Crag, praised the idea of a central stove around which groups would gather naturally and spontaneously, so making talking together about the day's work and the prospects for tomorrow easy and acceptable for everyone.

The plan included a large central living/dining area with access to small bunkrooms, showers/toilets, and a kitchen for self-catering. The building was set in a clearing in the Brathay woods with views through to the Langdale fells. The project was made possible financially by two generous initial grants. The first was from the IT Fund (chairman, Lord Hunt), which made a grant of £18,000, the largest the fund had ever made, and through the personal interest of Lord Pilkington and his special concern for St Helens, a second grant, of £13,000, was made by Pilkington charities. The St Helens Borough Council made an interest-free loan of £5000. An important contribution was made by Community Industry in St Helens, a scheme for providing practical training in the building trades for young unemployed people. At the cost of the timber

Eagle Crag during a course with disabled participants.

only, wall sections (both external and internal) were prefabricated in St Helens and transported to Brathay for erection on a site prepared by a local builder. After many delays, the Eagle Crag centre opened in September 1981.

New opportunities

With the opening of the new centre, Greenaway and Lesley Partridge (soon to be Mrs Greenaway) were appointed as tutors in charge. A new brochure described the resources of Eagle Crag and the promise of the links with the Centre for Youth, Crime and Community (CYCC) at Lancaster University, notably in developing a corrective curriculum to deal with young offenders. The blending of the CYCC's 'hard' skills in confronting delinquency with Brathay's 'soft' youth work skills foreshadowed important advances. Ideas that had begun in the Hall courses were now transferred to this far more challenging environment with great success. However, other demands on CYCC's tutors, as well as programming difficulties, prevented much joint action, and so Brathay was left to develop and expand the IT work on its own.

But if the original links were weakening, others were taking their place. During 1982 and 1983, there was a wide circle of new interest and bookings from IT groups in Cumbria, Liverpool, Manchester, Nottingham, Oxfordshire, three London boroughs, and Barnardos.

Decline in IT work at Brathay

Unfortunately, the success was short-lived and the number of IT courses began to decline. The reasons for this are complex, but reduction in the funding available from local authorities played a large part. This was a time of financial stringency, and it was not enough to argue that a course was a cheaper alternative to something else. In those hard times, even the cheaper alternative had to be pruned. The relative cost of doing the same work elsewhere was another factor. A National Youth Bureau directory for 1982 lists 23 outdoor centres providing facilities for IT residentials, many of them charging less than Brathay.

Changes among visiting staff also caused problems. As Smith observed, it was not easy for social workers to translate themselves into the Brathay ethos and come out unscathed. Teaching styles needed to be modified and understanding on both sides increased, common ground needed to be found between the approach of the social workers and that of the Brathay staff. Those who sponsored the IT courses also made changes. Many local authorities started to train social workers to run their own courses, which would ultimately make Brathay (the original catalyst) redundant. This is a not unfamiliar pattern and, in the broad view, not necessarily to be regretted. An indication that this was happening was the number of independent lets of Eagle Crag in the later years.

At the Brathay end, there were worries about the on-campus mix. Much of Brathay's income now derived from high quality management courses and, although they used separate buildings, contact was inevitable. Was it right to expect all users to be as altruistic as the founder? As a result of the IT courses, one perception of Brathay at the time was that it was some kind of Borstal, which in some senses it was. By 1985, the number of IT courses was down to three, none of them from St Helens. Nevertheless, Eagle Crag was in full use, as noted elsewhere.

THE RANK–BRATHAY PROJECT

This project began in Knowsley, a borough of Liverpool near St Helens, and Brathay's association with the young people of that area and their youth leaders was to some extent a follow-on from the IT work. Although there was no real connection between the two, the motivation was the same, a desire by Brathay to see its approaches to youth work applied in an area of particular need.

The original initiative for this project came from the Rank Foundation in the summer of 1982. Its representative, Larry Parsons, felt that Brathay's skill at leadership training could be useful. At a time of rising unemployment, especially in the north, and especially among young people, this

A youth group from Bradford in Eagle Crag.

was to be a pilot project to devise a programme that could be replicated elsewhere to identify and train young people with potential for leadership and voluntary service within their own community. The Brathay tutor assigned to this work was Jon Rigby, and his role, in the words of his report, was:

...to act as a training consultant, developing a training policy and structure based upon Brathay's approach to development training, which would eventually become self-supporting. By the end of the project, the trainees and trainers are to be wholly responsible for their own training and development. A major aim of the project was that it become redundant, demonstrating that...it can be 'given away'.

The project began in 1983, using Eagle Crag as the base but with much of the work also taking place in the home borough. Some of the trainee youth leaders who took part made the following comments:

Karen, 24: *The involvement of Brathay in the training element of the scheme has been a great asset, developing people's strengths when they didn't know they had anything to contribute.*

Andrew, 21: *Brathay has made a tremendous difference by helping them develop a team and by enabling them to raise social and work issues for discussion and analysis. But I would have liked to have received more skills training in outdoor pursuits.*

The Rank Foundation provided much of the funding for this project, supplemented by money from Brathay's own resources. The scheme was a very economical one and the amounts spent were tiny compared with the cost of the government's Community Programme (for the unemployed). And the project produced good results. Within Knowsley, there was an improved input to youth work, and, more importantly, more than 35% of the participants gained permanent employment compared with the average from other schemes of under 10%.

Knowsley and Salford

One of the intentions of the Knowsley plan was that it be replicated elsewhere, and a similar scheme was begun in Salford, Manchester, in 1985. But whereas the Knowsley plan had been linked to just one agency, the Manpower Services Commission (MSC) Community Programme, the Salford plan aimed to draw in the Church, the unions, the statutory and voluntary youth services, the MSC, the Sports Council, and industry. Brathay was also involved in another similar project in Newcastle upon Tyne, linking up with groups using the MOBEX scheme, an offshoot of the Young Explorers' Trust, which had been co-founded by the Brathay Exploration Group (see Theme 3).

All these projects were successful and those involved thought they would work elsewhere. Rigby ended his report on the Knowsley project thus:

The Rank–Brathay project succeeded in Knowsley; it is also working in Salford. I believe it will work in any part of the country. It is a national solution.

But despite its success, the scheme was taken up to only a limited degree. The vagaries of MSC funding and the ups and downs of the employment market meant that delicate plants of this kind were easily trampled under foot.

GOVERNMENT TRAINING SCHEMES

By 1978, youth unemployment was becoming a major issue in the UK and the government came up with various schemes to try to solve the problem. Brathay's first contact with these schemes was the conversion of the derelict Old Brathay barn into an accommodation unit (see Theme 4). Derrick Spragg was on the Brathay training staff at that time, but in 1979 he moved to the National Youth Bureau at Leicester where he was given the national brief of preparing the way for a residential element to be included wherever possible in the Youth Opportunities Programmes (YOPs). As a result, in 1981 Brathay, among others, began running one-week residential YOPs courses.

Appointment of a development officer

The YOP and Unified Vocational Preparation (UVP) courses came to Brathay at a very opportune moment since growing unemployment meant that fewer employed youngsters were being sent on courses. The numbers eligible for these government-funded courses were vast, so Brathay set up a completely new operational wing in 1982 in anticipation of these developments. Spragg returned from Leicester as development officer to take charge of this wing, which had its own (government-funded) mobile administration block. Soon Spragg also had responsibility for developing Brathay as a model Accredited Training Centre (ATC) for training leaders for Cumbria (and beyond) to run youth projects for the various MSC schemes. The ATC courses were also open to teachers, and this gave Brathay a valuable foothold in schools through which it could help them to develop new approaches.

Although there was some measure of financial expediency in taking on all this government-funded work, a positive spin-off was that many of Brathay's methods were becoming very widely disseminated. Spragg had been at the heart of these developments nationally, and he was now able to see that Brathay's best practice was known about and adopted far and wide. This was

gratifying, but the hoped-for financial rewards of working for government projects did not materialise. The MSC paymasters drove a hard bargain and the rules of the game were frequently changed. With such a large potential market for youth residentials, many other centres were also in the market for this work and Brathay, where the first tenet had always been top quality, found itself being outbid. Consequently, by 1986 Brathay had lost much of its youth work and had turned its attention to leader training through the ATC scheme. But even this work was lost in 1988 when the scheme was wound up.

The Rural Enterprise Programme

Into the gap left by the demise of these other projects stepped the Rural Enterprise Programme, partly funded by government but supplemented by a major grant from the Gold Fields Environment Trust. The aim was to help the long-term unemployed in outlying areas to develop their skills so that they could move into self-employment or return to further education or jobs. There were a number of elements to the scheme but Brathay's particular contribution was personal skills and confidence development two days a week. Unlike most Brathay courses, this was non-residential, with students coming from all over Cumbria.

   The scheme ran from 1986 to 1990, when it ended because of a shortage of funds in the recession. Like many such schemes there was great 'fluidity' in the numbers taking part. Sometimes people left because they had got jobs, but in other cases, unlike the well motivated trainees sent to Brathay by their employers, course members failed to continue because they felt little incentive to travel a long way to join something that might lead nowhere. It is hard to assess its overall effectiveness but, as far as approach is concerned, the project report says:

...in the harnessing of development training, which is Brathay's special expertise, to the counselling and guidance necessary to achieve its objectives...the Project stands virtually on its own nationally in the enterprise field.

OTHER COURSES

Courses for the young disabled

During the 1980s, Brathay held a number of courses at Eagle Crag for young disabled people from schools on the Wirral. Staff had the bright idea of using a drama theme (in association with the Gog Theatre Company) in which the youngsters would be put in the position of having to find ways of helping a person who was in great need, thus reversing the roles that disabled people often find themselves in. The scenario of each course created a new world with new ways of behaving, in which the dangers and challenges were simpler and more manageable for the children. It was a world in which they were there to help each other and all had something to contribute. Such approaches are commonplace now but were innovative in the early 1980s. Comments from participants included:

If I could try and get up to the Castle [Hardknott] then I can try and walk on my callipers when I get home.

Didn't think I'd be able to fit in...but the things we did made me feel just great.

The Eagle Project

This was the name of another series of courses, run during 1988, aimed at bringing able-bodied and physically disabled young people together to live, work and explore for a week. In true Brathay manner, the work involved them in the planning, played on their strengths, and got them doing new things, then learning and reviewing. One group included six totally wheelchair-bound youngsters, two who used a wheelchair occasionally, two people who could only communicate

through wordboards, two deaf people, two people who suffered occasional seizures, one with an artificial leg, and one who needed feeding. Such courses can be very demanding and the staff ratio, with much volunteer help, is very different from a conventional course. The costs can also be high but financial assistance was provided by benefactors. One young person who experienced the course summed it up thus:

...being aware of each other's needs, taking on many personal challenges from climbing a rock to feeding someone else, friendship, exploring their fears, not being afraid to ask for help or saying when it wasn't needed. Enjoyment, friendship, success, and rain!

The Prince's Trust Volunteers

Brathay has undertaken an increasing amount of work in association with the Prince's Trust Volunteers in recent years, and one such project was described on pages 7–11. The Prince's Trust Volunteers programme offers young people aged 16 to 25 the chance to develop basic skills such as decision making, communicating, and problem solving through team work in the community. The programme is open to anyone, but the majority of participants are unemployed. The courses are run by a variety of organisations, termed franchise partners, from colleges and universities to the Youth Service and British Nuclear Fuels Ltd. The role of the Prince's Trust is to set the pattern, to find partners, and to ensure the standard and quality of the programme. The first week, in the home area, is an introduction to the programme, to the team leaders, and to each other. In the second week the teams go to one of a variety of outdoor locations where the aim is to build confidence, trust and leadership skills. Brathay Hall is a popular choice for this segment. A 10-week placement follows, typically with a voluntary organisation to execute a community project.

Longtown Adventure Group

This is one of the latest of Brathay's youth work projects, and the following account considers the outcome of the 1995/96 course.

A group of youngsters that had signed on with the Carlisle Youth Service to take part in a series of residential activities at Brathay and elsewhere had come back to Brathay, a year later, to the august atmosphere of the Founder's Room, to give a presentation on how it had all gone. The presentation was their own idea, a thank you to Brathay for making it all possible.

It was very clear from their manner and enthusiasm that the year's activity had transformed their lives. How many youngsters of that age would have the confidence to put on an evening like this? The setting and the format could have been for adult management. Indeed, it had strong echoes of an event only two weeks previously when, in the presence of Lord Whitelaw, Brathay had gained its Investors in People award. But these were 13- and 14-year-olds, getting up in front of adults, going to the oak lectern and recounting what Brathay had meant to them. One said:

It gets me off the streets. I like doing the work, doing something worthwhile, a chance to take responsibility because I'm now chairperson of the group. You get on. It's good practice having to go to meetings and trying to raise money.

After the formal bit (which they loved and adapted to with ease), they made a point of going among the guests, who included a county councillor, county officers and a representative of the Brathay trustees, telling them lots more about themselves and taking them through the display of pictures of their life at Eagle Crag, their raft-building, and their canoe expedition on Loch Sheil.

The youngsters' parents, were equally pleased at the results of the course. Comments included:

The group has really changed her for the better. She's more confident and independent.

He has grown up a lot and he can organise things now.

Jane has gained invaluable experience in learning to work in a group, to work out problems and not just give in.

THE BRATHAY APPROACH

What lessons have been learned at Brathay from all these very varied youth programmes? Greenaway says:

Many of the skills we developed for the industrial trainees (young and not so young) were then transferred to our work with special groups of young people...these youngsters were ready to pick up what we were trying to do and gain benefit.

Spragg maintains that the work with unemployed young people, just as much as the management work, had helped to focus minds at Brathay on what development training is all about. The contrast between the Brathay approach and that of schools and colleges of further education (the only other approach most youngsters would know) is striking. Spragg sums it up thus:

Traditional approach	The Brathay way
Subject-based	Learner-centred
Passive	Active
Teacher	Facilitator
Facilitator	Self-development
Course programme	Modular/needs-led

He added:

Whereas so many of the other training schemes assumed that kids had nothing and knew nothing at the start, on a Brathay residential we start from the position where we assume that all people have got ultimate potential, and it's just a question of releasing it. If you give people confidence and self-esteem and belief in themselves they will learn what they need to learn.

Another distinction is that whereas the traditional approach to learning is very structured, especially now that the national curriculum specifies the content of teaching and levels to be reached for standard attainment tests, the Brathay approach helps people to cope with unstructured situations – such as finding themselves dumped on a hillside with no clear map to guide them and no easy recipes to follow – a real bonus in today's society, which demands that people be able to cope with the novel, the unknown and the unexpected.

THEME 7:
THE EVOLUTION OF DEVELOPMENT TRAINING

Brathay is generally underestimated because it doesn't blow its own trumpet. But the fact is that the whole outdoor management training industry was born here at Brathay at that time [1971]. Today, in the mid-1990s, there are something between 50 and 100 companies at work in this kind of management training. And it all started here. It was a most significant development. And I can't think of a better birthplace.

Professor John Adair

Development training has long been used by leading UK companies as an integral part of their training programmes for employees of all ages and status. It also has an increasingly important role to play in encouraging a more effective transition from school to adult/working life, a process that is now of special concern with the shortage of real work, the traditional mark of having achieved adult status.

Development training is about learning by *doing*. The active participation of all course members within their capabilities is expected, while relationships formed within the group and between the group and its trainer are of key importance. The trainer's role is not to teach but to ensure that the individuals gain the maximum amount of learning from the situations experienced, and that they relate this to everyday life. Throughout a course, during formal and informal group meetings and review sessions, the trainer encourages the group and the individual to review and evaluate the learning that has taken place, and to consider how that learning may be effectively applied in the future.

When people have completed a Brathay course they should have:

- increased their self-confidence
- improved their understanding of others
- acquired a sense of achievement
- broadened their horizons
- gained an understanding of the need for good communication and improved their personal communication skills.

To achieve this, programmes are carefully constructed to stretch the individual, both physically and mentally, in a variety of testing situations in which it is always safe to fail. In this way, individuals become aware of strengths and weaknesses and begin to understand how they react in different situations and under different pressures. They learn how to make the best of their abilities and what their weaknesses are, how to enhance strengths and compensate for weaknesses by matching with others in the group.

Brathay courses make use of a variety of projects, about half of them out of doors, to present new experiences and introduce new skills. A selection is made from screen-printing, drama, conservation, boatwork, raft-building, a mountain day, climbing and many other activities. Projects are designed to look at leadership, teamwork, mutual support, planning, use of time and resources, and communications. They also introduce responsibility for self and for other people and equipment. The individual learns through working with his or her team that relationships are important, that embarrassing situations have to be coped with, and that compromises may have to be made if there is not to be continual conflict within the group.

These processes help the individual to develop good judgement, a positive outlook, the will to overcome obstacles, the incentive to develop skills appropriate to need, and a real sense of responsibility for action. Above all, course members learn that the learning process itself is never finite.

A recent article about Brathay in *Human Resources* magazine puts it rather more opaquely:

Learning by doing shifts the onus from trainer to learner, emphasises self-reliance and embraces the power of teamworking. It fits well with the business culture of the late 1990s. Based on the principle that changes in behaviour result from experience, development training is intuitive and empirical, and since it focuses on the individual and on group processes, not tasks, it can be used liberally in any organisational context to address cultural, attitudinal and emotional issues and to develop emergent human competences.

THE BEGINNINGS OF DEVELOPMENT TRAINING: THE FIRST ADULT COURSES AT BRATHAY

There was a steady move towards working with older age groups between 1971 and 1991. Adult courses began in 1971, and, like so many of the beginnings at Brathay, they came about as a result of personal contacts. As we saw in Theme 5, Brathay had been working with the Industrial Society since 1969, using John Adair and his action-centred leadership (ACL) in the new-style Responsibility at Work courses.

Peter Prior was the recently appointed managing director of H.P. Bulmer & Co., the cider manufacturers from Hereford, and he was anxious to bring a new approach into the management of the firm. At that time, management training courses were usually of the chalk and talk variety in armchairs in comfortable hotels. Prior wanted something that included action and physical challenge. He sought help from the Industrial Society, and its director, John Garnett, put him on to Brathay.

Prior himself was no stranger to the training world. He was an ex-military man who had won the Croix de Guerre in the D-Day invasion of Europe. He had been in charge of an Army leadership school, and when he moved to Bulmers he brought a fresh, vigorous and unconventional approach to the job. He believed in the enlivening power of leadership, saying:

Leadership is a way of thinking, of getting people to do the things necessary to achieve a desired end. It is based on truth not prejudice; questioning assumptions; good observation of people and their reactions. Leaders show a preference for innovation, a belief in change and are always flexible in their approach to problems.

A Brathay course was consequently planned for Bulmers, and its in-house magazine, *Woodpecker News* reported on it thus:

It's 7 o'clock on the first morning. Rain is falling steadily. 'Right, lads, off to the ropes.' He meant it. Under David Gilbert-Smith, the Bulmer training officer, were 25 men of varied ages and states of physical fitness going through a course that threatened to deprive the company of a good proportion of its senior managers. Lecture and discussion sessions were the hard core of the course with the principles of Action-Centred Leadership driven home with fervour. These principles were later to be applied in many other outdoor schemes.

The rain gave way to glorious sunshine and we actually started to enjoy the bruising, leg-wearying, blister-inducing tasks. People we had previously linked only with their functions in the company suddenly became personalities as we fumbled with figure of eight knots to make a mountain rescue stretcher from an unwilling length of nylon rope.

...the objective was to carry out a search for two 'accident victims' lost in the wildest part of the fells and bring them to safety. The exercise included sleeping out in the open. Came the dawn and the poetic beauty of the sunrise was spoilt by mumbling noises from the scattered field of polythene bags as we woke to face inquisitive mountain sheep...

Was it all relevant to our daily problems at work? Those who took part unanimously say YES. We learned about people. People we thought we knew. Comradeship, unselfishness, charity – old fashioned words it's true – but in Brathay's setting they ring still more true.

Another view of that course comes from one of the delegates, Malwyn Owen, looking back 20 years later.

I remember it all well. It's still big in my mind! Just before our final night, I said to the warden, Denis Freeman, 'We shall never be the same again'. And he said, 'And neither shall we!'. It was all very democratic. And when you got your turn to lead you could boss your own boss about. It gave me perspective, taught us not to be submerged by the job, and to look at it clearly. Brathay was such a new environment and we were asked to face completely new situations. And I came back feeling great, that I could tear anybody apart...Peter Prior was the biggest cultural change Bulmers ever had.

Bulmers took the trouble to advertise the success of its course, and it was probably their initiative as much as any that stimulated interest among other firms. A second Bulmer course was held later in 1971 and was open to participants from elsewhere. The following view of that course was written by a *Financial Times* reporter whom Prior had invited along:

Does it work? It certainly improves communications inside Bulmers. It was difficult to believe that this was actually a collection of people only connected through their workplace; by the end of the week they were a close band of brothers. Peter Prior is certain that it works. He can already refer to an executive who attended the first course and who changed from being virtually impossible to deal with to a sociable co-operative member of the management. He can also point to the fact that the company's sales of cider have almost doubled.

Overcoming the challenges of barrels and planks on a management course.

Two more Bulmer courses were held annually over the next three years and took an increasing number of people from other firms. At the same time, Brathay was offering similar courses to the Bulmer model to individual firms such as ICI, GEC Machines and the John Lewis Partnership.

Then, in 1974, came a bombshell. Prior proposed that Bulmers take over Brathay and run it as a management training centre. There was clearly an expanding market for this sort of training, he reasoned, and where better to do it than Brathay? Although it may not have seemed like it at the time, in many ways the suggestion was the biggest compliment possible to Brathay's training methods. Nevertheless, Brathay had to refuse the offer. The place had been founded with the prime aim of training young people, and turning it over to adult work would clearly have been a violation of its Trust deed. However, there was nothing wrong, it was felt, with having a *proportion* of adult courses, particularly if those adults were in some way helping to bring on young people. Brathay staff, with the backing of the Industrial Society, clearly had the right skills for this work. And the recent Bulmer experience had shown that those skills were transferable to the adult world of management training.

The consequence of declining this offer was that Prior, with the help of Adair, set up the Leadership Trust, running courses from a base at Ross-on-Wye. It went on to become a very successful enterprise that attracted much attention and stimulated the great expansion in outdoor adult management training that has taken place during the past 20 years. Despite this loss of custom, Brathay continued to offer Leadership for Managers courses in association with the Industrial Society.

STAFF CHANGES

Director of training

Denis Freeman retired in 1975 and Kit Chambers came to head operations at the Hall. The title of warden was dropped and Chambers was given the new designation of director of training. He was a keen mountaineer and rock climber who had been an Army helicopter pilot before making a good living flying between the new North Sea oil rigs and Aberdeen. But he found the work unfulfilling, and although coming to Brathay meant a very big drop in salary, he never regretted it. 'The job was thrilling. I had a great team of tutors, creative and experimental, bursting with ideas,' he says. Chambers' team was an interesting one. It included Tony Bradburn, an ex-SAS man, full of grit and very inspiring, John Drabble, an ex-submarine commander, and art teacher Charles Whitehead. Brathay thus maintained its balance between physical and creative activity.

Chambers and his team believed passionately that Brathay's best hopes for the future lay in devising ever more attractive courses for people in industry who were going to be leaders, giving them self-confidence, skills in teamwork and communications, and instilling in them the importance of always taking a cool clear look at their progress. 'For us, the mountains and lakes were just teaching aids. These provided the experiences, but the really important thing was interpreting the experiences accurately,' Chambers commented.

Director of marketing

Another new post, that of director of marketing, was created in 1975. Not only was Brathay now trying to sell a wide variety of courses, rival outdoor centres were beginning to see the possibilities of manager training, and it was therefore time to adopt a professional approach to selling the product.

The job went to Ian Swanson. Although only 30 years old, he was already experienced in marketing and business practices having worked for a Sunderland company that manufactured paint for ships. Swanson had grown up in London and developed an early passion for rock climbing. At 17 he did a course at Eskdale Outward Bound, when Roger Putnam was warden. It was a revelation to him. 'It made me realise that there was more to me than I'd ever thought. It gave me a complete sense that the responsibility for my life was mine and not someone else's,' he

says. Disillusioned with selling paint, the Brathay post came at a providential moment for him. Like Kit Chambers, Swanson had to take a big cut in salary but in return for a huge improvement in his way of life. As he puts it, 'the chance of Brathay felt to me like a new beginning, a mission'.

Communications

Another arrival at that time was Martin Crocker, an actor who joined the team with a particular brief to develop communication skills. He recalls putting the new ideas into practice:

With Charles Whitehead I worked up all sorts of exercises using party games and blindfolds, planks and barrels, suddenly confronting them with new problems. We were constantly trying out new ideas. I'd put one of them in an empty room, blindfolded, and then get him to go and describe it as best he could to the others, who then had to draw a diagram of the room based on what they were told. Then the course would study the results and have long intense discussions about it.

COURSES FOR INDUSTRY AND COMMERCE, MID-1970s

The mid-1970s were years of high inflation, rising unemployment and poor productivity, so persuading firms to spend money on training was a big challenge. Brathay offered something for everyone. There were the 19-day Responsibility at Work courses for 17–21-year-olds, aimed at personal development, plus the 14-day Preparing for Leadership courses for 18–23-year-olds, for development of leadership and potential in young employees. There were also the nine-day Managers in Action courses for those aged up to 50 years old, the successor to the Bulmer courses, plus tailor-made courses for specific companies (see below). This marks the time when Brathay started to run several courses simultaneously (now standard practice).

BRATHAY TRAINING OPPORTUNITIES IN 1979

During Chambers' time the title Brathay Training Opportunities had been adopted to cover all the Brathay work that did not come under the Field Study Centre or the Exploration Group. Andrew Brown took over from Chambers in 1978, at a time when it was clear that the emphasis on management training was paying off. There was a strong government emphasis on training and various Industry Training Boards had been set up, through which it was intended that such work should be encouraged and co-ordinated.

During 1979 company courses were on the increase. Brathay ran courses for GEC Machines, the John Lewis Partnership, the Post Office, the Chemical and Allied Products Industries Training Board, Marks & Spencer, ICI Plastics, ICI Mond, and Caterpillar Ltd. Brathay also assisted in courses for Union International, Imperial Group, Courage Ltd, ICI Petrochemicals, ICI Nylons, and Allied Breweries. All in all, 1979 was a most successful year, and Brown commented thus in the year's annual report:

The number of courses and those attending was the highest ever (12,640 delegate days). We drew our students from an even wider spectrum of industry and commerce with particularly strong support from the retail and distributive sector. Brathay training is only fully effective when it is recognised as a significant element in a continuing programme of education and training. An encouraging aspect of the year has been the growing number of client companies who understand our work and how best to relate the Brathay experience to everyday working life. An essential element in the evaluation and follow-up has been the ability of the Brathay staff to communicate effectively with company training and personnel staff. This has been achieved at all levels through an increasing number of visits by company staff to Brathay and vice versa. The net result has been a constant review of course content and a commitment to maintain the relevance of Brathay training to the world of work.

The increase in the numbers attending courses had improved Brathay's financial position. The reliance on subvention from the Scott Trust had fallen from 35% to just 11%, and the management work itself was making a satisfactory surplus. Much of this change in fortune must be put down to Swanson's work as director of marketing, demonstrating that Brathay must never neglect the importance of this aspect.

QUANTITY AND QUALITY

Good projects continued into 1980 in all areas of Brathay. In the management training wing the open courses (Responsibility at Work, Preparing for Leadership, Managers in Action) and the new Supervising for Results were all fully subscribed, and 14 courses were run for individual companies or groups, including new names such as Newcastle University. Assistance was given in courses for at least eight other groups including National Park Wardens and Bolton Wanderers Football Club.

Quantity was one thing, but Brathay had always seen the *quality* of its training and presentation as of paramount importance. In 1981, Mike Housden took over as director of training. He came from an industrial training background with GEC, and Derrick Spragg, one of his staff, recalls his insistence on high professional standards in all that Brathay did, a necessary response to the expectations of clients at that time.

The next 15 years were to see many changes in the staff and organisation at Brathay (described elsewhere under the appropriate themes), but the development training courses for industry (as they were now called) remained strong throughout. Although this work involved a fundamental widening of the age range of the delegates and a great deal of soul-searching about Brathay's chief role (see Theme 8), it was these management courses and their continued popularity that enabled Brathay to remain at the forefront of the educational and training world.

THE DEVELOPMENT TRAINING ADVISORY GROUP

In 1977, the Development Training Advisory Group (DTAG) was founded by Brathay, Outward Bound and Lindley Lodge, born of a desire to co-ordinate the new approach in the principal charitable outdoor training establishments. One of DTAG's early roles was to give evidence to a House of Commons Select Committee on Youth. Full members now also include Endeavour Training, the YMCA, Fairbridge, Bowles, and the Ocean Youth Club, while the Trident Trust and the National Association for Outdoor Education (NAOE) are associates.

DTAG exists to 'exchange ideas, experience and information about development training; promote the concept of development training and its use; help uphold standards and improve the quality of development training; undertake joint action and initiatives whenever appropriate, e.g. in development projects and in relation to government policy'.

Its statement on who development training is intended for parallels Brathay's own approach:

In the past, programmes of development training were run mainly for apprentices, and other young trainees, of major companies, and this is still an important client group. When funds permitted, this provision was extended to unemployed young people on YOP, YTS and YT schemes. Some programmes are now aimed at young offenders or those at risk; others focus on deprived inner city communities. Schools are also clients, with outdoor adventure and activities, and also cross-curricular themes like citizenship and personal and social development, now forming part of the national curriculum.

In addition, many managers and supervisors now undergo development training as an integral part of management development strategy, and for building management teams. This client group includes senior executives from industry, commerce, local government and public sector organisations. The programmes for this group are geared to support the implementation of corporate strategy, with less emphasis on personal development. Regular clients of the DTAG organisations include most of Britain's leading companies and many national agencies.

Thanks to DTAG, Brathay was funded by the Manpower Services Commission (MSC) to set up the Cumbria Association of Residential Providers (CARP) in 1985, with the aim of raising the quality of development training in all the many centres in the Lake District. Subsequently, DTAG was asked by the MSC to establish other similar supportive associations in other parts of the country, using CARP as the model.

THE JOHN LEWIS STORY

Among the firms who were attracted to using the 'new style' Brathay, none stands out more prominently than the John Lewis Partnership. With its unique management structure, the firm owns 23 large department stores plus the food chain Waitrose. Its house magazine not only keeps staff, or partners as they are known, in touch, but enables anyone to write in, make frank comments, and expect a reply. So it is entirely through the writings of that house magazine that the John Lewis involvement with Brathay is related.

June 1973, report from director of personnel to chairman
From time to time in the past, young partners have been sent on residential character training courses and among these has figured the Brathay Hall training centre. Sponsorship of such courses has, however, been on a fitful basis and it was thought that consideration ought to be given to offering such places regularly to a larger number of partners.

November 1973
Earlier this year I agreed that we should undertake an experiment by asking Brathay to run, especially for the Partnership, two courses, each for about 50 young partners with a syllabus tailored to the Partnership's needs. Our own trainers will co-operate in the running of these courses...

April 1974
(Announcements) During March we ran a two-week course for some 50 young partners. Our intention is to repeat this in November and continue on a similar scale for the next two or three years. It was clear that the response of the partners has been outstandingly favourable.

(Letter) Sir: Is it true that since the last course at least two of the section manager participants have left the Partnership to take more challenging managerial jobs outside? Did we pick the wrong people? Or did the course overstimulate their self-confidence and cause them to be dissatisfied with their previous lot?

(From the John Lewis Partnership general inspector) I was invited to a course following some comments about safety. I found that the arrangements and, more importantly, the attitudes to safety were beyond criticism...Brathay, with its special ethos, does seem to be something more than just another management training centre.

October 1976
The Governors of Brathay wish to extend their management training and conference facilities. The Partnership has offered to provide this accommodation (24 single/double rooms with facilities) on the basis that it will be available to Brathay for the six winter months. For the six summer months it would be, for the Partnership, 'an amenity centre in the north'. The site of the proposed building is a large walled garden at Brathay. The Council may feel, as we do, that the attractions of this project are enhanced by the fact that it will help Brathay in its future development and in its work of helping young people develop their abilities.

June 1978
(Re the 'amenity centre in the north') The trustees of the various trusts on the Brathay side also approved the project in principle...Unfortunately, although there has been no shortage of enthusiasm and good will on both sides, there have been complications...Legal difficulties then arose on the site...lawyers have still not completed the agreements...Original expenditure of £250,000...now risen to £400,000...a further increase to £480,000. In the circumstances it seemed sensible to consider alternatives...Ambleside Park Hotel...£300,000...need to act quickly... [In the event, the John Lewis Parternship bought Ambleside Park Hotel.]

December 1980
(Letter) Sir: There is a Brathay course called 'Preparing for Leadership' to which many different firms send employees...The Partnership, however, block books a whole course, thus limiting the scope...What wisdom lies behind this policy?

(Reply from chief training adviser) When we wished to send 100 people a year it became necessary for Brathay to run separate courses to accommodate us. Partners may not mix with employees from other organisations, but they have the advantage of working alongside colleagues from a good cross-section of the business: department stores, supermarkets, central offices, warehousing, transport and production units. The most important aspect of the training is the way people use what they have learned when they return to their jobs.

November 1983
With two courses a year, attended by about 50 partners each, that means that to date around 1000 young people have been invited to test their strength in the various practical trials that the courses include. [Their attendance remains a Brathay Record.]

One anecdote that did not appear in the in-house magazine concerns the adaptation of the John Lewis Partnership slogan 'Never knowingly undersold' by the members of one course. To the bottom of their course programme they added the words 'Never knowingly underworked'.

Brathay's work with John Lewis continued for many years. The early experiences with the company were used to draw in other firms such as GEC, helped by John Lewis itself, which went to the trade exhibitions and conferences to tell of the work. The partnership was reinforced in 1981 when the original John Lewis staff link, Mark Hope-Urwin, became a governor of Brathay and, later, its chairman. Courses continued but, as in so many developments pioneered at Brathay, the bulk of the work has now been taken over by the firm itself.

RECENT MANAGEMENT TRAINING WORK

Many other firms have also used Brathay extensively over the years. Some of their recent experiences are related below.

MANWEB

One company that has made very considerable use of Brathay's Development Training courses is the Merseyside and North Wales Electricity Board (MANWEB). Its links with Brathay go back many years and a number of the senior staff recall coming to Brathay long ago as youngsters on the four-week courses. The firm was privatised in 1990 and decided that all its senior managers would benefit from special, carefully tailored courses in leadership and teamwork as they shouldered new and greater responsibilities. In 1991, David Hannah, the MANWEB training manager, put together a programme that included a development training residential experience. At the suggestion of one of MANWEB's non-executive directors, Richard Morgan, who is also a Brathay trustee, the company chose Brathay for this element. The one-week courses proved to be such a success that the senior managers were soon demanding similar events for their own staff.

And so began a long sequence of courses in which the accumulated wisdom was able to 'cascade' down through the different levels and departments of the company: 60 senior managers had attended courses, followed by 400 middle managers, and then approximately 1500 cross-functional staff. By 1995, something like half of the company's total work force had been through the Brathay experience.

MANWEB's personnel director, David Vernon-Smith, says:

Brathay has been tremendously useful to us. We always found the trainers there very flexible and helpful in designing the special courses we needed.

Bill Tubey, currently their resources group manager, is also supportive:

For most people this was their first taste of that type of work. If you ask any of those people, they will all remember their Brathay week because it was so good, because we learned so much. There are certain things about that week that are imprinted on my mind for ever. One of them was the blindfold rowing. It just really brought it home to me that if you are in a boat, blindfolded, and somebody tells you to row, you don't know whether you are going forwards, backwards, doing it well, or too fast or too slow, whatever. But if you've got a good leader who tells you, that's right, you're doing it well, that's the right thing to do, it makes you think about how people sometimes feel at work. Exactly! We could just see that. We were talking about people back at work: a cable-jointer or a labourer and we tell them 'just dig!'. We don't really tell them enough about it all, and where they are. We needed to develop our attitude to people, and what we can do for them along those lines. We all came away really fired up with what we'd learned in our new roles, in the new world we were moving into. It created a team spirit which I can remember coming out on one particularly difficult occasion. We had to make a collective decision on an important issue; for some of us it was painful, and there was a great deal of debate. After nearly an hour I can remember that the Brathay-type spirit started to come out and people were now very much working together, helping each other out of the trouble. We were now really a team. So, the course has stood the company in very good stead. People are now very supportive of each other and I think that's where it all started to come together.

Courses nowadays, particularly company courses, are focused much more closely on assisting the implementation of the strategy of that company. Many of them will use a week in the Lakes to enable them to look afresh at that strategy. People open up in a remarkable way after a walk in the fells or after some task in which they have seen their colleagues in a new light and had to work as a team. Tubey comments:

At Brathay we were brainstorming our way through some of the problems we knew we would have to encounter when we came back. We started putting the ideas together which eventually came out in our new Company Agreement – in terms of the things we wanted to do; in terms of the way we organised ourselves, staffing levels, and the customer service ethos which we wanted to start to drive through. This was a time when we were changing staff attitudes on how we dealt with our customers.

When asked why they had to go to Brathay to have such discussions, Tubey said:

It was because we were off-site, getting involved in all those physical things which really do develop team spirit, and because it was exciting and different, it all came together. We all came away with this very great admiration for the professionalism that we saw at Brathay in terms of the way that they dealt with us. We came away feeling this is a good professional organisation; maybe something we should aspire to in our own organisation.

One useful part of every company course was when one of the senior managers went up to visit them for an evening session to see how they were getting on. But this was more than just supportive; on those occasions people will really open up and get all sorts of things off their chest. One interesting aspect of sending so many people over a period was that those who had been (who were not supposed to let on about the projects they did up there) gradually got more in number and 'the buzz' that went round about the place was most exciting, remembering the good things and sharing the experiences.

The Rover Group

Few firms have made a closer link between company objectives and the team-building offered by Brathay than Rover. The following account is from a report in the Rover in-house magazine, *Transition*, on Rover's view of what took place in 1988.

When Geoff Evans was told to climb up a waterfall, relying for support on some colleagues at the top holding a rope and others at the bottom telling him exactly where the footholds were, he felt just a shade nervous. If you had poked your head over the top of the waterfall as he was climbing and asked him what all this had to do with building a better car engine, he might have suggested that you take your conversation elsewhere. In fact, as he discovered later, his exploits that day seem to have had a considerable effect on the development of the K series engine.

The K series is the first new engine design, for a small or medium-sized car, that Austin Rover has produced in 30 years. It is shrouded in secrecy until its official launch next spring, but is believed to be costing the company between £100 million and £150 million. But Austin Rover has a problem; the company was originally made up of a number of smaller firms and many people still felt more loyalty to their old group than to the wider company. There were also departmental barriers – some related to the former companies and divisions – and it had proved hard to get departments to work well together.

The programme they implemented, led by training design manager Barrie Oxtoby, is a marvellous example of training theory put into practice. It has wrapped up into one neat parcel all the ingredients which anyone who sat through a training conference listening to papers about the ideal world was ever told about: outdoor development training, open learning, on-the-job self-development, trainers acting as facilitators, people taking charge of their own learning, top management involvement and team-building.

After an introductory half-day with other colleagues and company directors, the 18 set off on a four-day outdoor development course to Brathay Hall in the Lake District. They came back transformed. The course was viewed by the participants as the key feature of the programme, the catalyst without which the rest would not have happened.

Tense moments in project planning.

They were pitted against the waterfall on the first day. They also climbed, walked, camped, boated and talked. A group of people who had been virtual strangers became, for four days, intimate friends. They admit there were arguments and tempers flared. But there were no major bust-ups. They learned to rely on each other, to be aware this was happening and to analyse their own relationships.

'The feeling of having done that as a group and trusted someone, the confidence we felt as a group and as individuals, was terrific,' said one of the members. 'At the end of the four days we were a bit shattered and had worked hard physically and mentally. The atmosphere in the group was unbelievable; we would have taken on anything or anyone. If you could have bottled that spirit and determination and sprayed it all over everyone else in Austin Rover we would have had 110% of the market by now.'

The Halifax Building Society

The Halifax Building Society is another firm that has made good use of Brathay. Its personnel and head office director, John Lee, comments:

For the last 10 years the Halifax has sent a group of young trainee managers to Brathay for a week. This week forms a small but important part of a two-year management training programme. The programme is designed to equip people to understand the retail financial services business. Much of the programme is about products, processes, systems management and customer service.

This is where the course at Brathay dovetails in so well. It provides a safe and supportive environment in which participants can learn about achieving the tasks through and with others. Our trainees are stretched by the programme; some of the tasks can represent a significant personal challenge. The sense of achievement and the realisation of what can be achieved when a team is focused on the objective and works together to reach it is a powerful learning experience.

THEME 8:
COMMERCIALISM OR ALTRUISM?
THE PERIOD 1983–1991

THE VISION

In common with many charities Brathay has to contend with the often conflicting demands of altruism, on the one hand, and commercial necessity, on the other. Both demands have a place in any organisation that claims to have vision, but managing the balance between them can be very challenging, as we shall see in this survey of the crucial period between 1983 and 1991.

The governing body and the Brathay Hall trustees

In mechanical terms, a governor is something that controls the speed of an engine to ensure that it fulfils its function with maximum efficiency. A governor itself has no power and can only work properly when the engine it controls is chugging along smoothly. Over the past 50 years, Brathay has been served by a variety of different bodies, called, variously, councils, management committees, hall committees, advisory committees and governors. Many prominent people have served on these committees and their contribution to the success of Brathay has been inestimable. But their role has not been an easy one since the 'engine' they sought to control was complex and, as we have seen, sometimes changed its character and even its component parts.

As a charity, Brathay also has trustees, whose main function is to ensure that the place is run in accordance with its Trust deed. For much of the past 50 years the trustees were also members of the larger governing body. This changed in 1987 when the trustees became a separate and additional layer of the Brathay administration. (There is also a further 'layer': the Francis Scott Trustees, who administer the founder's largesse; they have no role in how Brathay is run but are landlords of the Brathay estate.) It has been argued by some that these layers are necessary so that those who are guardians of the ideals (the Trustees) are not encumbered by the day-to-day administration of the organisation, being able instead to leave this to a larger (governing) body. However, this multilayered structure also has weaknesses, as Brathay was to find out in the late 1980s.

THE EARLY ALTRUISM

In the earliest days, the altruism came from the activities of Dick Faithfull-Davies, who, we are told, was no businessman. His altruism had therefore to be contained within the commercial possibilities offered by Francis Scott, his businessman patron. But even within the generous limits set by Scott, it was necessary to make some gesture towards making ends meet. When the regular summer Holidays with Purpose courses started, for example, it was commercialism as much as altruism that led Brathay to offer its hospitality in winter to convalescing boys. Later, when Old Brathay became available, apart from the three years when it was used for the Oxfordshire schools courses, we see a series of largely commercial-led attempts to develop it as a conference centre, although none of them really worked.

The Scott Trust backing

Throughout those early days, in fact for the first 25 years, the chief and almost unimpeded drive in Brathay was the altruistic desire of those running the place to provide young people with an ever-widening range of opportunities for self-discovery. The money for all these enterprises came almost entirely from Scott and his charitable trust. Brathay (the estate and all the buildings)

belonged to the Scott Trust, and every year it picked up the bill for as much as 50% of the full running costs. By 1969, the Scott Trust's share was down to 42% (including capital grants), but this was still a very large subvention. This was quite deliberate, however, since Scott wanted Brathay to be free to work the way he wanted according to his plan. He wanted it to be free to experiment, and it was this freedom that enabled it to establish its distinctive role in the world of outdoor education. Quality was all, and Scott wanted Brathay to be the envy of other centres. He wanted to see his money used to maintain Brathay Hall as somewhere that young people would remember with pride and affection. 'Give people quality surroundings and they will respect them,' was his motto.

His vision was of a centre whose staff and environment were of a high standard, that was in a glorious setting, and yet that was friendly, informal and supportive. Many of the 'students' came from uninspiring urban backgrounds and he wanted them to have a memorable experience. Over the years, his money helped to improve the place further with buildings of character: the boathouse, the theatre, the dining hall, Eagle Crag, the bunkroom dormitories and the barn.

Scott's munificence resulted in some perverse effects, however. His money was deposited in a number of trusts and, while he was fully in charge, he could 'steer' this money as seemed best for the latest project. But in the late 1960s, when Brathay sought greater control over its place of work, the Scott trustees decided not to hand over any of their capital assets to Brathay. So the Brathay trustees are tenants and any money they raise to improve the property benefits not the Brathay Trust but the Scott Trust. However much goodwill may exist between the trusts, Brathay has not inherited an easy position. Scott's declared wish was that his Trust should be the sole source of subsidy for Brathay to ensure its independence. In fact Brathay is now expected to find subsidy wherever possible, and can no longer expect to receive money from the Scott Trust as of right.

RETIREMENT OF BRIAN WARE

In the early 1980s, the era of the charismatic individual who could both personify the vision and draw in the income was coming to an end, and it was the moment for the governing body to assess its role in defining what Brathay was and where it was to go in the future. As the time of Brian Ware's leadership was drawing to a close, the fruits of Brathay's sheltered development were plain to see. Much had been achieved under the beneficent umbrella of the Scott Trust, and this was largely due to the vision and skill of Ware himself. When he came to Brathay in 1966, there was just the Hall, running four-week courses, and the Exploration Group (BEG) based in the huts in the woods. When he retired as principal 17 years later, work at the Hall had blossomed into a diversity of courses for all ages and for all levels of achievement, Old Brathay had become a flourishing Field Study Centre with attendances often exceeding those of the Hall, the BEG was running 17–20 expeditions a year, and Eagle Crag had been set up as a centre for young people with special needs. In terms of premises, there was also the development at Old Brathay barn, giving another 20 beds plus an impressive large meeting room, all brought about through an imaginative job creation project. There was the new dining hall and kitchen, and a new 2 x 12-bed dormitory on top of the hill behind the Hall. There was even Tiny Wyke, a 10-bed retreat for returning old boys, a project very dear to Scott's heart.

THE MARSH REPORT, 1983

There was euphoria at Brathay's success, but this alone would not carry it into the future. At Peter Scott's suggestion, the governors agreed that a professional study should be made to see how best to pass on Brathay's success to the world at large. John Marsh had been interested in Brathay since Francis Scott had brought him on to the management committee in 1950–51. He was director of the Industrial Welfare Society from 1949 until 1962, and retired in 1982 from the post of director general of the British Institute of Management.

Marsh's report began with praise:

Brathay is a success story. I am most impressed that Brathay is very active, broadly alert to the changes in the work and leisure scene, and is aware of rapidly advancing technological frontiers of our time. Brathay has emerged clearly and firmly as a centre of great future potential to the nation. Brathay has earned the respect of associated organisations nationally.

Marsh referred to the ups and downs of the Youth Service since the war and commented:

Brathay has not only survived, it is broadly viable, it has immense vitality and commands real respect amongst those in the country who know of its work.

Traditionally, Brathay had kept a low profile, quietly getting on with its work. Perhaps it was now time to change all that and 'go national', Marsh suggested. Of the effect of the Manpower Services Commission (MSC) and its like he said:

In an age when we realise that too much has been left to the state to solve or ameliorate the problems of our society, with the dead hand of bureaucracy often stifling risk and initiative, there is a clamant need for the voluntary principle in a democracy to be re-expressed and to re-assert itself.

Marsh was some 15 years premature when he anticipated some form of 'national social service'. 'If it comes,' he said, 'it would be a great pity if Brathay were not involved in the dialogue and was party to the formulation of 'what's to be done' and 'how it's to be done'. Brathay, as a laboratory and a power house, could well make a significant and practical contribution to these developments because it is flexible, pragmatic, and can speak from a success record with young people from different walks of life, and a wide age span'.

The Brathay philosophy

The first recommendation in the Marsh report was that Brathay should formulate a clear statement of aims. A long-standing governor, Bishop Launcelot Fleming, was invited to work this up after consultations with staff in all sections of Brathay. The resultant document is given in full in Appendix B.

The Brathay Extension Service

By 'going national', Marsh meant that Brathay should offer its services as a 'think tank' in the field of youth training, issue a series of punchy publications to inform the media, local and national, about its work, get represented on national and regional committees, spread the work widely, develop a consultancy service, play a more active role in getting money from government, local authorities, education bodies, other charities and, possibly, from what is now known as the European Union. To do all this he suggested setting up what he called 'the Brathay Extension Service'.

For a year after his retirement, Ware headed an embryo extension service on a part-time basis with some success. The work included:

1. The Industrial Experience (INDEX) Project initiated by Pilkingtons in St Helens for school leavers at 16. This pioneer youth training scheme (with 120 places annually) provided a useful transition to the world of work.
2. The Trident Trust (see Theme 6), a consultancy on the scope of development training, finding ways to extend personal and social development through outdoor challenge.
3. Education for Capability. In 1983 Brathay had received one of the first of these Royal Society of Arts (RSA) awards. Encouraged by this, in partnership with the RSA and Cumbria Education Committee, Brathay organised a two-day conference for over 50 delegates from all sectors of education.
4. Brathay Australia. During his sabbatical, Ware visited the Mountaincraft organisation in Melbourne. Its director had twice visited Brathay and his well established approach to development training (for managers and youth) was closely modelled on Brathay's. There was a strong wish to develop closer links.

Despite these developments, it soon became clear that Brathay had neither the resources nor the will to expand in the way Marsh was advocating.

The new Principal

Appointing the first new Principal for 17 years in 1983 was a major undertaking, but there was no shortage of candidates. The trustees appointed David Richards. Like many of those who played an influential part in the Brathay story, Richards was a teacher (of English) by profession. He had always enjoyed mountain walking in Scotland and the Lake District, but he had never been to

David Richards, front row, centre left receiving a cheque from Consolidated Goldfields

Brathay, although he had heard it spoken of with admiration at the Headmasters' Conference. He had also long nurtured an interest in 'the pastoral side of education and personal development'. He had served as headmaster of Hereford Cathedral School and then Portsmouth Grammar School, and thought it would be good to have a change. Not having been 'brought up' in Brathay and therefore not having seen how all the various bits had evolved, Richards was understandably confused by what he found.

My period as principal was at times wonderful, lots of high quality work was being done, with great enthusiasm, by a lot of wonderful people. But it was sometimes distressing as well, immensely demanding. There were stressful management difficulties because of the diversity of the work. Who was Brathay working for? Academic sixth-formers and university students? Urban kids at risk? Thrusting young businessmen? The inner city unemployed? Or all of them? And was that possible? We were trying to do a lot of very different things all at once, and when a small organisation is trying to do that you are like a juggler, struggling to keep all these balls in the air. It was particularly difficult for me because all these balls seemed to be valuable ones. But it simply wasn't possible to keep them all going, partly for financial reasons and also because it created a sort of culture-clash among the staff.

REDUCTION IN SCOTT TRUST SUPPORT

In 1983, the Scott trustees intimated that they would have to consider a reduction in the amount given annually to underwrite Brathay's work. Eventually, Brathay would have to stand on its own feet or obtain other funding. The trust would continue to contribute for five years to help build up an endowment fund, but thereafter there would be no more endowment money and no regular annual subvention. To some people this seemed an outrage. Wasn't the Scott Trust specifically formed in order to look after Brathay? But over the years the Scott Trust had widened its brief to embrace other concerns. In Kendal it was committed to improving cultural life by the provision of a museum and art gallery at Abbott Hall, and an arts and community centre on the site of an old brewery – the Brewery Arts Centre. It also had its own projects concerned with social needs and the disadvantaged, and these needed funds.

Two other factors may also have influenced the Scott Trust's decision. First it noticed that the management courses run at Brathay created a surplus and that that surplus could perhaps replace the Trust's subvention. Additionally, in the eyes of some Scott trustees, Brathay was doing work beyond its remit in the Trust deed, and they therefore saw no reason to underwrite that work. Second, the concept of tapering off the level of grants as a matter of policy was becoming a common trend in many charities and government-funded work at that time. The argument was that an organisation could become too dependent on support and become unhealthily reliant on it.

Brathay's defence of subsidy

The Brathay governors mounted a strong defence of their position:

1. Although it did adult work (and happened to be rather good at it), the main thrust was still with youth.
2. Youth work would always need subsidy from somewhere.
3. Brathay was charged to experiment, and such work can be financially risky and often loss-making.
4. If surpluses from management work were to cover all costs there would have to be a vast increase in that work, making it, in the eyes of some Scott trustees, even more unacceptable.

While the percentage of the annual subsidy, once 35–50%, was now down to about 11% a year, that still amounted to a large sum, being over £67,000 in 1982, and £51,500 in 1983. After adding in the amounts for special projects, and the contribution to the endowment fund, the amount given to Brathay each year could average about £90,000, about half the sum then available for dispersal by the Scott Trust. The thought of doing without this money or finding it from somewhere else was a daunting one. Financial stringency all round became the order of the day, and Richards had the unenviable task of looking at each of the Brathay operations and deciding not just whether it was a 'good thing', but whether it could in some way cover its costs. Financial viability was essential for survival.

In these difficult times, Richards was fortunate to have the backing of Clarice Rose as finance officer. Rose came to Brathay in 1968 and was to serve some 23 years in all. Brathay owes much to her calm manner and efficiency in dealing with many crises, and her firm hand on the purse strings was, in the end, much appreciated.

Closures

The first casualty was the Brathay Extension Service as it was clearly impossible to put any financial weight behind a new venture of that kind, however worthy. Nevertheless, Ware, typically, continued much of this work, driven by the momentum of a lifetime's mission. Thirteen years after 'retirement', he is still involved in projects that grew out of Brathay.

The Field Study Centre was the second casualty of the cuts, as described in Theme 4. While this may have made a cash saving, the overall effect on the usage of Brathay was catastrophic. In the four years between 1984 and 1987, the overall number of delegate days dropped from 26,000 to 16,000.

The national appeal

A national appeal for funds was launched in 1985, personally organised by Richards. He had previously orchestrated appeals for Hereford Cathedral School and Portsmouth School, so this was familiar ground to him. He knew that to attract funds it is essential to have specific projects. The focus of his appeal was to provide the resources for a range of courses for the young disadvantaged, courses that, like the Knowsley scheme and the intermediate treatment before it, had some residential elements but also links to the home area. Direct bursary assistance for people coming on such courses was also sought. Eagle Crag was to be extended to almost double its capacity (to 20 + 4 staff), and improvements and enlargements were planned for Old Brathay. Richards was fortunate in all this work in his assistant Audrey Hallowell. Recruited for the appeal, she stayed on as personal assistant to succeeding heads of Brathay, fulfilling a key role in the administration to this day.

Of the effort involved in fund-raising, Richards says:

If you believe in what you're asking for money for – and I very much believed in the value of Brathay's work– then you'll ask anyone. All I had to do was persuade them to come and look at what we were doing, and they would give.

He did much travelling and talking, and the results were gratifying: in two years, almost £750,000 was raised.

The split in the training team

In 1985, largely due to MSC demand, activity in Brathay was growing fast and, as it came in, the appeal money was quickly allocated. But as we have seen, Brathay now had to be more commercial in its approach, and anything that did not pay its way could not be sustained unless it could attract external subsidy.

When the Field Study Centre closed, there was a reshuffle of the remaining tutors. Those specialising in management training (now mainly for adults) became the staff of the Centre for

Leadership and Development Training based in the Hall. Those doing the youth work or youth leader training work became the staff of the Centre for Youth Learning, using Eagle Crag, Old Brathay and off-site locations. At about the same time, the title given to the staff who dealt directly with the 'customers' was changed again. The term 'tutor' was felt to imply that the person was the guardian of some knowledge that was being passed on. On the other hand, 'trainer', the new term, implied that the person was helping others to make fuller use of the talents within themselves. There is an element of both these roles in much of Brathay's work, but the term 'trainer' was more familiar to industry, now the main supporters of Brathay.

The aftermath

Richards left in 1989 partly, he says, because of what he felt to be the unclear nature of the brief he was getting from the various bodies controlling Brathay. It was also a time when many organisations in the training field were feeling the strain of the uncertain national situation. At the schools level, many local authority centres were closing, and those that embraced government training schemes too wholeheartedly could easily be caught out when the goalposts were moved. Richards comments:

My years at Brathay were very fulfilling. Lots of the work was new and exciting. But it was also very demanding, full of difficulties. A very complicated job.

THE DIVISION OF GOVERNORS AND TRUSTEES

Towards the end of Richards' time as principal, Peter Scott took the view that fully separating the governing body from the Brathay trustees would be beneficial. He argued, from his experience elsewhere, that this would make fund-raising more effective. However, in management terms this two-tier plan soon displayed the weakness referred to earlier. First, servicing it required a great deal of work, and more meetings for those at the hub. More importantly, it tended to distance the trustees from the decision-making on such matters as policy, planning, approval of budgets and the appointment of key staff. Since it is the trustees who are ultimately accountable for the consequences of these decisions, it is important that they should have a hand in them. Furthermore, they needed to be well informed for their role of mediating with the Scott trustees who, despite their earlier intentions, had not yet fully implemented their proposed reduction in subvention. The 'divorce' was thus a mistaken policy, and the longer lines of communication led to a decline in confidence and understanding between the Brathay trustees and their governors. This was to end, in 1991, in the replacement of both bodies by what is now called the council of trustees. Brathay, like so many of its commercial clients, had simplified its structure.

THE NEW CHIEF EXECUTIVE

In 1989, Judith Manifold joined Brathay to replace Richards, but with the new title of chief executive to emphasise the business, rather than the educational, aspects of the work, felt to be an important selling point at the time. Trained and experienced in personnel work, she came from Lancashire and had been one of the first personnel and training officers in the National Health Service, after which she was chief executive of the Merseyside Educational Training Enterprise.

She made changes to the names of the different departments. The Centre for Youth Learning became the Youth and Community Development Programme, and the Centre for Leadership and Development Training became the Management Development Programme. The gap between the two centres widened. The numbers on youth courses were declining and so the accommodation designed for young people was being underused. Old Brathay was about to go into mothballs. Those coming on management courses were now expecting a higher standard of accommodation than bunk dormitories (however well appointed). Rival organisations without a fixed base could simply block-book hotels. In response, Brathay also booked nearby hotel rooms, but a more satisfactory answer was the conversion of the dormitory block behind the Hall into 12 single *en suite* rooms. This was a costly exercise but it was justified on the grounds that it enabled Brathay to retain a foothold in the 'top' end of the management training market.

THE FINANCIAL CRISIS

Richards' fund-raising enabled much subsidised training for young people to be provided but it did not make Brathay any more commercially viable. And, whatever the altruism, the commercial imperatives had to be faced. Ian Swanson, then a member of the governing body, sums up the situation thus:

Judith Manifold hosts HRH The Prince of Wales on a visit to Brathay in 1990. (Photo by courtesy of the Westmorland Gazette).

Brathay's problems were largely self-generated. There had been a drop in sales, but we were not marketing sufficiently vigorously. Brathay had got itself involved in too many of the government's youth training schemes, which were expensive and bedevilled by the fact that governments often change their minds. Brathay still offered excellent courses, but it was not in organisational shape to cope with all the pressures. There was no clear overall policy, and no clear channels of responsibility and command. The different sections of Brathay were drifting apart from each other, separating and splitting. The staff were never, by the nature of the job, easy people to manage – young and enthusiastic, bright and articulate, committed idealists, desperate to be consulted and encouraged and considered, but seldom business-minded.

By now the decline in support from the Scott Trust was beginning to have serious effects. In 1988, on a reduced subvention of £60,000, Brathay had finished the year just £770 in credit. The next year it received only £30,000, and made a loss of £87,000 (i.e. a trading loss of £117,000). In 1990, Brathay was given just £20,000, the final annual payment from the Scott Trust, and made a loss of £18,000 (£38,000). Delegate day numbers were well down, partly because of the loss of the Field Centre, but also because of a general recession in business nationally. In 1989, leaving out the BEG, there were 9000 delegate days compared with 12,000 the previous year, and even that had used only half the capacity. The percentage of young people had also changed dramatically. In 1984, leaving out BEG, 89% of course participants were aged under 25, but by 1992 that had dropped to 28%. In fact, the decline in young customers was so great that Eagle Crag was also put into mothballs in 1990. As in any business, if trade declines, staff jobs are on the line, and Manifold had to make redundancies. Virtually all the 'youth' staff lost their jobs.

As a result of these problems, Manifold left in June 1991, and Brathay was forced to thoroughly reconsider its direction. However, it was to emerge from this difficult and uneasy period in better shape than ever before.

THEME 9:
RECOVERY

Adventure may be of the mind, of the spirit, of the imagination, as well as a physical experience; it should entail uncertainty of outcome and a degree of hazard, and most importantly, the outcome should not be predetermined; it should depend on the efforts, the judgement and the commitment of the participants themselves. In other words, they should manage as far as possible their own project, within a suitable framework.

Roger Putnam in *In Search of Adventure* (the Hunt report)

Brathay was not alone in having to face a crisis in 1991. A national and worldwide recession had begun, which many were reluctant to recognise. The altruism behind many of the youth courses could no longer be afforded, and the only money being spent on young people seemed to be on those in trouble, often interpreted in the press as 'adventure holidays for naughty boys'. With fewer people in jobs, there were fewer people wanting training courses, and so those offering courses (of whom there were now a great many) were themselves competing hard for work.

Although it was a time when many firms went out of business, Brathay was not on the brink. Thanks to the prudence of earlier years it had begun to build up a substantial endowment fund as a cushion against any serious downturn. As things turned out, even in 1991 Brathay broke even, but only because a very firm control was placed on all spending. The Brathay trustees, now renamed the council of trustees, were in sole control. They decided to set their house in order and to establish a clear vision of where they were going before appointing a new chief executive. A number of the trustees took on new responsibilities.

Sir Christopher Ball, who had chaired the trustees for a short time, felt unable to take on the increased burden that the enlarged role for the trustees would involve, however, and he resigned. The Honourable Andrew Hepburne-Scott, a relative newcomer, but one with a strong financial background, took his place, but had to retire because of ill health after just a short while. Mark Wolfson MP, a previous chairman of both the governors and the trustees, took over. Two former governors, Dr Bertie Everard and Ian Swanson joined the trustees and Swanson made a most generous offer to stand in, in an honorary capacity, as part-time chief executive until such time as a proper replacement could be appointed. The offer was gratefully accepted and for the next nine months he lived a demanding double life, dividing his time between his usual work (in venture capital) and guiding the complex Brathay operation.

IAN SWANSON

Swanson remembers it as a busy but also a thrilling period. The staff rallied round. 'I got a phenomenal response from the staff. They pulled out all the stops. Their commitment turned the situation round,' he says. Describing how he tackled this formidable job, Swanson says:

First, I set up a management team, five heads of department, who met each week to make the key decisions. Then I talked regularly to all members of staff, and that included the domestic staff, to explain what we were doing. Next, we put great emphasis on vigorous marketing, particularly for the management training side of our operations. Marketing was in a mess – key staff had gone, orders were dropping. Then I insisted on quality work. The crisis had gone on for months – things had got slack, tatty. And finally we tried to bring back Brathay's sense of fun. We were after something of the Dunkirk spirit – backs to the wall, we can do it. And we did.

Having ensured that the staff were satisfactorily looking after the day-to-day operations, Swanson's next task was to prepare a realistic five-year development plan. This concise but forthright document set the course for the future. The following extracts give a flavour of it.

Brathay is an educational charity...to provide young people with experiences which encourage their physical, moral and intellectual development...to investigate and research questions affecting this process...and to train people concerned with the development of young people. Brathay has only a small investment income [and so] it must generate funds sufficient to sustain and develop the residential centre and its staff. The objectives and strategies...are designed to ensure that the Trust achieves:

1. *fulfilment of its original purpose*
2. *sustainable long-term financial viability*
3. *widespread influence upon development training.*

Objectives

1. *Independence through achieving a substantial operating surplus from development training in the commercial market to subsidise the youth work.*
2. *Balance: 10,000 residential days per annum for young people under 25, of which 33% are for subsidised and/or disadvantaged groups.*
3. *People: attract the best, at all levels.*
4. *Quality: buildings, facilities, equipment and service of the highest standard in the field.*
5. *Influence: reputation as the leading, most innovative organisation in development training.*

Despite the challenging target, and no mention of begging for outside support, the turnround in morale was immediate, and everyone worked all out to make it a success. This was a very clear example from within Brathay of how effective leadership can rapidly achieve change. What Brathay taught its clients, it now had to do for itself.

BRIAN LIVERSIDGE

There was a very strong field of over 700 applicants for the post of chief executive. A choice was made and the successful applicant, Brian Liversidge, took over in May 1992. As a young man he had briefly served as a police officer in Blackpool before spending more than 22 years as an officer in the RAF Regiment ('more a soldier than an airman,' as he puts it). His own officer training period had given him an early introduction to John Adair's ideas about 'the functional approach to leadership', which he later put into practice enthusiastically when he spent two and a half years at the Officer Cadet Training Unit at Henlow in Bedfordshire. He was not a mountaineer or rock climber, but he kept himself fit playing Rugby Union and cricket, and running marathons. He was also a keen motor cyclist. RAF service took him to many parts of the world including the USA and the Middle East, and he rose to the rank of Wing Commander. He loved the life but, in 1989, feeling that he needed a change, he resigned to join his brother in running a small engineering firm. Then, in 1992, he saw the advertisement for 'the best job in the Lake District'. He was delighted to meet Adair at the selection panel, and to get the job . Four years on, he says it has been very hard work but he has no regrets at all.

Liversidge is a big man and he exudes confidence. His manner is direct, and he is very much on top of the job, which he has found a fascinating challenge. 'I like the diversity,' he says, 'working with the whole range of people, from deprived inner-city kids to the senior managers of the big, successful companies. It's never boring.' He works intensively and his personal assistant Audrey Hallowell, says his one serious fault is that he drives himself too hard and doesn't know how to give himself a break.

He has great faith in the value of the work done at Brathay:

Brathay spawned a whole new industry in management training. It was here at Brathay that it all began. And the work for young people, which is what Brathay was started for, is still needed as badly as ever. Far too many people are growing up blinkered and narrow, locked into their videos and TVs and computers, unaware of all the things the world has to offer. It's worse nowadays for the men. Young women can get jobs, but a lot of young men can't. It's all too easy to give way to despair. The need is still there: to open horizons and to give them pride and confidence.

An early priority was to get youth work re-established. Although all but one of the full-time youth staff had been made redundant the previous summer, many were still in the area and there was an increasing availability of well-qualified freelance trainers with experience in this field. In the event, Eagle Crag never closed down and, with freelance staff, some youth work continued throughout the winter. In anticipation of the upturn, in February 1992 Swanson called a seminar of the key freelance people, and prepared the ground for Liversidge to take over. A key figure at this seminar was former staff member Phil Whitehurst, who had served for 10 years in Brathay's youth department. One encouraging statement from that seminar was:

Brathay is seen as the natural leader in development training for youth and community groups and its innovations over the years have resulted in a very high reputation for effective work.

Another, more chastening, message to come out was that many people had deserted Brathay for cheaper centres. Brathay had overpriced itself.

Brian Liversidge.

Revival at Old Brathay was not so swift. Ever since the demise of the Field Study Centre in 1986 there had been no steady use of the place for a clearly defined purpose. One idea, although not new, was that it should go 'up market' and become a base for senior management training. But the cost of conversion seemed high and, in the recession, there was no guarantee of a strong client base to justify the high cost. Another idea, canvassed by the Exploration Group and their supporters, was that, in association with other partners, it should become some sort of international centre for environmental studies, bringing together explorers, scientists, overseas volunteers and environmentally minded business firms. But this was not a time to take risks on a completely new venture and, anyway, lease obligations apart, Brathay was not sure that it wanted to part with any of its sovereignty. In the end, Old Brathay was let out to students from Ambleside's Charlotte Mason College as a means of paying the maintenance bills until such time as Brathay's results could create the funds to use it once again.

THE REVIVAL OF YOUTH WORK

Although Swanson had set high targets for the number of young people attending courses, the income to subsidise these young people (apart from the industrial apprentices) had first to be raised. As a result, the lowest number of young people since 1948 came to Brathay in 1992, fewer than one-tenth of those attending in the late 1970s. This was the low point, but one from which Brathay was to rise in a dramatic manner and with a strength all its own.

In early 1993, Brathay appointed Steve Lenartowicz to head the new Youth Department. He had a background of teaching in local education authority centres, at Outward Bound and in independent centres with courses aimed at the full range of people from managers to those on government-funded youth training. Among his more personal achievements was canoe-camping with his three young children in the remoter parts of Canada.

Under his leadership, youth work at Brathay rose in 1993 to 4302 delegate days (compared with 2357 in 1992), and this rise continued through 1994 (5954 delegate days) and 1995 (8006). The 10,000 delegate day target is now in sight. In 1996 Eagle Crag is in full use, and much of Old Brathay has been refurbished so that two youth courses can take place

simultaneously. The subsidy for this was covered by the surpluses plus a substantial grant from the Francis Scott Charitable Trust. There have also been generous grants from the TSB Foundation and the Rural Development Commission.

The nature of the work is currently very wide-ranging, but Brathay cannot do everything. One view is that it should concentrate on training the trainers. Nevertheless, it does not want to develop a 'training college' remoteness, and it plans to continue to work directly with large numbers of young people themselves. Judging by the joy that so many young people get out of coming to Brathay there can surely be little doubt that this is valuable work.

In 1994, the youth training programme included special courses for under-25-year-olds from many parts of the UK, including Carlisle and the industrial towns of west Cumbria, Merseyside and north Wales, Garstang, Bradford, Doncaster, and several London boroughs. Many of those attending were subsidised by local education authorities, charitable trusts and businesses, in addition to Brathay's own built-in subsidy. The Merseyside police are very active in arranging Brathay courses for local teenagers (see below), and British Nuclear Fuels (BNFL) and UCB Films have sponsored Prince's Trust work for west Cumbrian unemployed. The Francis Scott Trust, the Dulverton Trust and Marks & Spencer are also prominent among those who give their money generously in support of Brathay's youth work.

The Police and Youth Encouragement Scheme (PAYES)

It was after the horrific murder of toddler James Bulger by two young boys that Merseyside police decided to see what Brathay might be able to do to help. 'That crime highlighted the dangers of children out of control,' one of the senior officers said. 'It showed how easily truancy can slip into something much more serious.'

In January 1993, Merseyside police sent a group of high risk 12–14-year-olds from the Bootle area on a week's course at Brathay, accompanied by some officers. The kids and the police got on well together and greatly enjoyed themselves. Much more importantly, the course proved far more effective than anyone would have dared hope. A year later, not one of the youngsters who had attended the course had got into trouble with the authorities again, which compared

favourably with probation: Home Office statistics show that over 30% of children put on probation re-offend within a year.

Detective Chief Superintendent Albert Kirby, one of the senior Merseyside police officers shattered by the Bulger murder, became a great enthusiast for Brathay training. He attended another such course in February 1994, and told a *Sunday Express* reporter:

I passionately believe this is the best way of preventing another James Bulger tragedy...It is a better way forward than locking people up and throwing away the key. The idea is to teach youngsters how to take responsibility for themselves and others. Teamwork and trust are vital. When children are abseiling down a rockface they are forced to rely on colleagues for survival. Hopefully, they will see the bobbies who are helping them as friends rather than enemies.

The Youth At Risk courses

Youth At Risk is a national charity that runs intensive rehabilitation programmes for young people with serious difficulties in their lives. Brathay's partnership with it began in 1993. Despite Brathay's past success in helping young people in need, it was not without some hesitation that this new type of course was taken into the programme. At the time, Brathay did not have a strong team of resident youth specialists, and this work was very much at the 'hard end' of catering for young people's personal needs. On the other hand, the Youth At Risk staff were bringing to the partnership a highly experienced team whose leaders (at that stage) came from the USA. They had been very successful in attracting support and funding (including some from the Francis Scott Charitable Trust) for what has to be a very expensive operation.

Some 20 to 30 young people are each paired for a year with a trained volunteer. Each meets regularly with his or her volunteer and specialist supporters, as well as with each other, but the year begins with a six-day residential challenge, which is where Brathay comes in. Before Brathay became involved, there had been only one Youth At Risk course in the UK. Brathay has now participated in six courses and the pattern looks set to become a regular and valued part of the annual programme, accounting for about 5% of Brathay's total work.

Youth At Risk literature states:

The objective of the six days and of the programme as a whole is to support the development of self-awareness and self-esteem necessary for the young people to make positive choices in their lives.

The approach is highly confrontational, although caring, adopting the slogan 'tough love'. On the first day at Brathay:

Participants are invited to consider that more may be possible in life than they had previously thought, or than might be predicted, based on their past circumstances and experiences. They look at the unseen possibilities for their lives. This opens avenues of thought and action for them.

The work during the Brathay segment consists partly of challenging activities around the estate such as on the ropes, the high wall, and – a Youth At Risk innovation to Brathay – the 'pamper pole'. This last involves a daring (but safe) leap from a high pole while being encouraged by the crowd below. It is all about trust, and the lessons from these activities are then related to life's problems and opportunities. Those on the course also spend time in the course room where they are led in discussions by highly experienced course leaders.

Criticisms of this work range from 'too confrontational' and 'too American', to 'too expensive'. In fact, although now developed to a very high standard in the USA the approach includes elements that were included in early post-war Brathay courses. Full credit must go to the American Breakthrough Foundation, whence the scheme originated, for venturing to tackle an area of need from which many people would shrink. As for the expense, the costs of the course

must be weighed against the costs to society if these youngsters fall into serious trouble. Another creditable aspect, and one from which Brathay is learning, is the use of volunteers. Both for the residential, and for the full year, it is volunteer helpers who have been trained to see the youngsters through the activities and the traumas that come with the ups and downs of success and failure. Significantly, seven of those volunteers on the most recent Youth At Risk residential were people who had themselves formerly been 'youths at risk' on previous programmes.

Does it all do any good? The Dartington Social Research Unit is currently carrying out a two-year evaluation, and the residentials have been observed by a wide range of professionals with an interest in social welfare. The founder of Youth At Risk, Ben Rose, says:

The reaction from these people has been more than positive. Youth At Risk has many letters on file from outside observers attesting to this.

After attending four days of a course and visiting events during the year, John Huskins, a former inspector in youth education, says:

The residential training is highly professional and effective in reaching its intended purposes.

Brathay's input to these courses has been steadily increasing, not only in providing staff, but also in influencing the style of work with, as Huskins observes:

...greater emphasis on small group work as its potential for learning is recognised. Increasingly, the Brathay experience of using the outdoors for development training is being incorporated into the residential.

This type of work tends to attract publicity, some positive and some negative. In 1995, the *Mail on Sunday* newspaper expressed interest in the work and was invited to visit a course. The headline 'Boot Camp Brain-Washers' vividly summed up the gist of the resultant article, some of which was so inaccurate as to make the organisers wonder whether the reporter had really had any interest in the facts. The contrast between that article and a meeting at Brathay four months later with Trevor Phillips from Channel 4 television, was most marked. Phillips came to glean information about the work of volunteers for a Royal Society of Arts lecture and heard nothing but glowing reports directly from participants in another Youth At Risk course. The sad thing about the 'Sunday newspaper school of journalism' is that so many people read it, leaving Brathay and Youth At Risk with the tedious – and costly – job of seeking to put the record straight. The chief probation officer for the Inner London Probation Service said on the matter:

This scaremongering article is a discredit to investigative journalism and a betrayal of an organisation which seeks to give fresh hope to young people's lives.

MANAGING AND MARKETING THE BRATHAY OPERATION

The overall day-to-day running of operations at Brathay is the responsibility of Andy Gill, the operations manager. Gill has been at Brathay for 10 years. His background is in vigorous outdoor activities such as climbing and caving. He worked as a trainer for a local authority and then at Ullswater Outward Bound School. Of the current developments he says:

There's a new and clear-cut controlling structure. Management training pays the overheads and helps to subsidise the youth training.

It is clear that all the staff, whatever their role, are committed to the new pattern of work and understand what Liversidge calls the *duality* of the work. Gill says:

There's lots of scope for further expansion as companies change their attitudes, working habits and styles. We work closer to our clients now, trying to meet their special needs. They've become much more sure about what they want from us, and very much quicker to let us know if they're not getting it. Our courses are much shorter than they used to be – three days is about the average now – and more concentrated and focused. Our trainers range in age from their late 20s to their mid-50s. There are more women than men at the moment. They're usually here about three years before moving on. There is a continuing analysis of training methods so we can become even better.

It is clear from the ups and downs of attendances over the past 50 years (see Appendix C) that strong marketing has been an essential factor in Brathay's recovery. Although no one has ever accused Brathay of complacency, it is a fact that if an operation is heavily underwritten by a regular and generous subvention there is less need for people to go out into the hard world and 'sell' the place. And in the days when Brathay was a pioneer it tended to rely on satisfied customers to go out and do the publicity for it. In today's world, however, it is not enough to be good and certainly no use being modest. You must shout it out, make them hear, and pull them in.

In the early days of the recovery, Brathay was fortunate enough to draw in one or two key industrial/commercial customers who were sufficiently impressed by the work to send a great number of their staff (see Theme 7). Repeat business of this sort is a useful indicator of success, and in 1995 this was standing at 80%. However, open courses are not drawing much support any longer. They have been reduced to some 15% of the total management business, and courses are frequently cancelled. The conclusion from this is that firms no longer want someone else's idea of a course, however good, and prefer to negotiate their own tailored package.

The marketing department is run by Andy Dickson who has graduated to this post via many other parts of Brathay. He has specialists in his team, but each trainer also works as an 'account manager', looking after his or her group of clients, giving the best possible service, keeping in regular contact, and putting all information on to the computer. New customers are found in a variety of ways. The best is word of mouth from existing customers, but Brathay is also active in seeking out firms in this potentially vast market, both by advertising and taking stands at the national business training conferences. Among those experienced in the business training world, the perception of Brathay is a favourable one. Courses are sometimes pricey but they are considered to be 'top of the range'. Brathay is aware, however, that not everyone can afford top of the range, and is always seeking ways of restructuring the courses for other markets while maintaining the quality.

It must be admitted that Brathay remains little known among the wider public, and even among those who support one or other of its arms there may be no clear overall perception of what it stands for. In a recent interview, Philip Sadler, former principal of Ashridge Management College, commented that whereas everybody had a perception of what was meant by Outward Bound and the Leadership Trust, the word Brathay simply signified a place. 'If only they had changed to some new name in the 1970s, things might have been very different,' he said.

THE BRATHAY EXPERIENCE, 1995

The following account is by the local writer Alan Hankinson.

One evening by Lake Windermere, a most astonishing spectacle could be seen. Four women and two men, dressed in home-made clown costumes, stood in line and sang a simple song, clearly of their own composition. They had coloured balloons, wore large paper hats and decorated paper blouses that proclaimed their name: 'The Air Circus'. It was all very light-hearted and decidedly amateurish. Mercifully perhaps, their sole audience was a group of eight men, who stood by a raft they had made from logs, planks and plastic barrels. When the song was over, the audience clapped and cheered and then launched the raft, getting wet in the process. They then clambered on board and paddled it out a few yards to establish its lake-worthiness.

This was the climax of an action-packed day for 14 executives of AVCO Trust plc, one of the UK's leading consumer finance houses. Dick Love, their vice-president (human resources/quality) writes: 'We have been using Brathay for three years for a tailored course designed to translate everyday work issues to another environment. The experience has enhanced personal awareness of strengths and also assisted our company in developing cross-functional activities.'

The course was directed by Margaret Rock, one of Brathay's trainers. She devised the course and said its aims were: 'to provide a development programme which will enable individuals to become more aware of their own style of working and its impact on other team members, and to equip them to work more effectively in situations where there is ambiguity, constant change and a need for co-operation between groups of people'.

The AVCO delegates had already done three long days of intensive training before the morning of Thursday 8 June dawned. By then they had tackled several problem-solving exercises and met physical challenges like 'the ropes course', an elaborate sort of obstacle course that involves moving quite high above

the ground by way of a variety of ropes and logs. They had learned rudimentary skills that would be needed later in the week, such as screen-printing, juggling, and ways of lashing planks together securely. They had worked as teams on various complex projects. They had spent a lot of time discussing their efforts and what they had learned from them, where they had gone wrong and why. The previous day they had climbed a mountain near Ullswater, which some of them found tough going, and then spent the night in a rough cottage. Now, back in Brathay for breakfast, they were all slightly groggy from this pressure and excitement in an unfamiliar environment. Today they were confronted with the final and vital test of the course, a day-long exercise called 'Helter-Skelter'.

Rock explained the exercise. They were a company that specialised in delivering goods and messages for people, often in unusual situations. The company would start operating at 10.30 a.m. with an initial capital of £630, which would gain interest at 10% an hour. Their target was to make a profit of at least £2000 by 5.30 p.m. A number of key customers used their services regularly, and there was a potential new customer, a Ms Alder, who was expecting a telephone call from them at 10.45 a.m. To run the business they had the use of a room with tables, chairs, sheets of paper, etc. and a direct telephone line to 'outside'. The roles of the various customers were played by Rock and two other Brathay trainers, Sulwen Roberts and Ann Alder, assisted by two 'technicians', Bruce Robinson and Ian Wilson, whose chief responsibility was to make sure safety rules were observed at all times.

Rock described 'Helter-Skelter' as 'a complex exercise involving change management, quality, working in flexible teams and finding out customer needs'. It was only a game of course, and the money was only Monopoly money. Despite this, and despite their early morning grogginess, I was amazed at the whole-hearted enthusiasm with which they hurled themselves at the challenge.

At 10.30 prompt the phone in their 'office' rang, and the day's business had begun. The customer who rang was having some trouble with spiders, and so the team found that their first exercise involved delivering six members through gaps in a rope 'spider's web' without touching any of the ropes. For this they received a fee of £50.

Exercise precipice

Next came an exercise called 'Precipice'. Roberts played the part of a customer who was offering a fee of £60 for the delivery of an envelope. She stationed herself on a ledge of a side wall of Brathay Hall and the team of six had to get the envelope to her from the front of the building, eight yards or so away, by edging along a narrow ledge. It was only two feet above the ground, but for the purpose of the exercise it was 'the precipice', and if anyone fell off and touched the ground then the whole operation had to begin again.

The team considered the problem for a few minutes and then a small agile young man, who clearly enjoyed this sort of game, set off carefully, edging his way along the 'cliff' flattening himself against the wall of the house. There was just room for his splayed feet to shuffle along, but there were no holds for his hands. So a second man, considerably taller, reached across to help hold him upright. The leading man soon reached a place where the ledge widened sufficiently for him to turn round and lend a hand to the next man. There was another such narrow traverse to be negotiated before the first man was close enough to pass the envelope to Roberts.

Mission accomplished, and they began to congratulate themselves on £60 well earned. But this was premature since Roberts was far from satisfied. The envelope was badly crumpled! There was a photograph of her nephew inside and it was ruined! Did they call this quality service? She expected better than that for £60. A brief altercation followed. They had not been told there was a photograph in the envelope and there was no 'Please do not bend' warning. They were sorry for the damage and it would not happen again. But the customer stood firm, and they finally agreed that £35 would be a fair fee. The exercise had been about pre-planning, team-work, helping each other, and keeping cool, rational and polite in unfamiliar situations and in the face of unexpected setbacks.

All morning the group was busy earning money. Six of them, for £60, undertook what they call the 'Trust Fall'. One stands on the edge of a low wall, three feet or so from ground level with one's back to the others who stand ready to catch the falling body. One man asked to go first because, he said, if he had to wait he knew he would never do it. 'It goes against everything my mother taught me,' he explained. It calls for some nerve, and trust in the others. The faller is advised to keep his body as rigid as possible. The catchers do all they can to reassure and encourage him. Finally he falls, is safely caught and feels great. They all did it and experienced immediate elation, the joy of having done something you did not think you would be able to do.

Another group of six, all men this time, were commissioned to get a small parcel safely around the ropes course, observing all the safety rules but under time pressure. They all wore helmets and climbers' harnesses. They did it, but took longer than they should have. They handed the parcel to their customer who opened it up and cried out: 'You've broken it! It was an egg!' The fee of £100 was reduced to £80.

All the time Rock was devising new commissions for them, chivvying them that they were not earning fast enough, shifting the goalposts to keep them on their toes. She got me involved, offering them £300 if two of them would grant me a 20-minute interview on what they felt about the course. They said they would do it, but only for £1000! That was clearly ridiculous and, after a few minutes haggling, they settled for £300.

I talked to Dave Boss who is head of in-service training at AVCO's Reading HQ, and Ian Menthorp, the Scottish district manager. What were they hoping to get out of the course? Boss said he was hoping to strengthen his self-confidence, improve his team-working ability and perhaps find new ways of managing people. Back at the office they were all, one way or another, in positions of leadership, used to giving the orders. Here at Brathay the leader changed continually. They had to learn to take orders, work with others. At least two of them (he did not name them) both natural and forceful leaders, were already greatly changed. Ian confessed that there had been one moment, when they were struggling up the mountain, when he began to wonder what they thought they were achieving. It was painful and seemed pointless. Then it became apparent that two of the women in the party were struggling even more than him. So he turned to encouraging them and stopped worrying about himself. And when they reached the summit the world seemed very different.

They both agreed that it had been pretty intense. Both had been surprised by the things they had managed to do; physical things, and the efforts of thought and self-control that had been demanded of them. They were impressed by their trainers. 'You can put your trust in them,' they said. 'They work hard at making us work hard.' Dave said that they ran their own internal training at AVCO, playing business games and the like, but they ended at 5 p.m. 'Here, they go on till 9.30 or 10 p.m.,' Ian said. 'I've slept like a log, shattered!' The continuous pressure had led to some friction in the group, but also to a great feeling *of camaraderie. They stressed that the course was much more than just a few days of intense activity. Before they came they had discussed and written about what they were expecting to gain from it. When they got back they would be required to write about the experience and there would be more discussions.*

The scenario for the day warned the group that one of its senior directors, a Mrs Rock, would come and speak to them at midday about 'the latest thinking about the future of the company'. When she came the news was a bombshell! The company was being totally reorganised. They had got too comfortable and settled in their ways. They were not earning anything like fast enough. It was time for a shake-up. So their original profit target for the day was doubled to £4000. They must look for bigger projects, come up with brighter ideas and sell them harder. They could break for lunch now and start working out their strategy for the afternoon. And it had better be good!

After lunch, they seemed to be a long time getting cracking; they needed to do a lot of discussion before the strategy was agreed. Sitting at the receiving end, waiting for the phone to start ringing, the Brathay staff began to wonder if they had decided not to bother any more. But no; when they did get going, it was with a vengeance. They undertook several commissions that could be accomplished quickly to raise the money needed to buy equipment. They were charged for everything, and if they ran into debt 15% interest would be charged hourly.

Six of the men hurried off to do a 60ft abseil from a nearby tree, with a small bonus for giving a downward ride to Rock's teddy bear. Then, to my astonishment, five men earned £100 for climbing up the fearsome 'pole'. The 'pole' is a free-standing telegraph pole about 25ft high and a foot in diameter. There is a ladder to get you half way up, then a series of little metal steps hammered into the trunk to give hand-

holds and foot-holds. At the top, with no further hand-holds, you just have to get one foot on to the top and step up boldly. It is all perfectly safe as you have a well secured top rope firmly attached to your waist harness. If you fall off, the rope will hold you in mid-air and you will be rapidly lowered to the ground. So it is merely a matter of persuading your legs that there is nothing whatever to worry about. Once at the top you have to shuffle carefully around through 180 degrees, trying to stop your legs from juddering, and then leap for a trapeze a few feet away. Then you will be lowered to the ground, feeling marvellous. To make matters worse, they told me, the tiny platform has a slight but noticeable wobble to it. They all did it, some more elegantly than others, to roars of encouragement from their colleagues. They were all on a considerable 'high' when they returned to their office HQ.

By this time, a new well heeled customer had been found, and there was the prospect of some real profit-making opening up. There was to be a big celebratory party by the lake. The new customer was wanting a raft built that would carry up to eight people and display a banner. It had to be floating by 4.30 p.m. There was a lot of haggling about this on the phone. They wanted to charge £6220 for the job, but the customer said that £3000 was the most she could offer. It became clear that further projects would have to be included. They chose to go for producing some kind of lakeside entertainment, designing a logo and making festival T-shirts. They realised that the profit from all these would take them past their target of £4000, so they finally rang the customer back at 3.15 p.m. to say they would build the raft for £3000 but that it would not be ready until 5.15 p.m. She accepted and the deal was clinched. The group then split up into various teams and completed all the tasks.

It was not quite the conclusion of the course for the AVCO delegates. They were allowed to relax that evening with a farewell celebratory dinner, but the next morning there would be a lengthy discussion on a Career Development Action Plan. After lunch they left Brathay, strengthened perhaps in certain ways, certainly enlivened.

This was not just a five-day course. Long before it began, Brathay consultants had been to AVCO headquarters to ascertain what the company wanted and to work out an appropriate programme. Now there would be further visits after the course to ensure that what had been achieved at Brathay was being firmly followed-up.

Hankinson also attended a course run by Brathay for the Manchester Business School. This is his account of the experience.

In the past decade, Brathay has built up a close relationship with the Manchester Business School. It had been developing training along similar lines to Brathay, laying great stress on analysis and discussion of learning experiences. Brathay was the context in which the students were now to have these 'learning experiences'.

The students come from all over the world and right at the start of their course they are taken to Brathay to begin to get to know each other and to feel at home in the UK. This was a very large course for Brathay. There were 134 students and it was to be an intensive three days. Many of them were travelling abroad for the first time, but they seemed to be settling in quickly and happily.

I went to watch the climax of the course on the final day. The course director was Ann Alder, a veteran of this type of training and a great believer in its effectiveness. She had eight other Brathay training staff to assist her. The students, from 25 different countries and four continents had been split up into eight groups with 16 or 17 in each group. They had been kept ferociously active during the first two days and now, on the last morning, they were involved in a wide variety of 'money-raising' challenges. (In this context, 'money' is the points they score for the various challenges appropriate enough for future businesspeople!) These challenges included raft-building, solving a 'murder', writing song lyrics, and tackling a ropes course. With the 'money' raised, they could purchase the materials needed to make their 'presentation': a three-dimensional work of art on the theme 'valuing diversity', and portraying their own wide diversities and demonstrating their newly acquired team skills.

They were given a very short time to work out their presentations and to rehearse them. A brief period of apparent chaos ensued, but it was creative chaos, full of enthusiasm and invention. The results were remarkable for their wholeheartedness, their ingenuity and their variety. Some were artistic, some musical, some verbal and dramatic. Each one was effective and yet entirely different from the others. In every way diversity was displayed and celebrated. Everybody seemed delighted.

Peter Barrar, the Manchester man in charge of the students' two-year course, watched it all happening. He said: 'I believe very strongly in the great benefits of these courses. The students work. They begin to get to know each other. They start thinking seriously about problem-solving and working as a team, about their own roles in the group, what they do best, and what they are not so good at, the areas where others tend to excel, the importance of standing back to consider what they are doing and how they might do it better. And it gets them to see the Lake District and to realise that there is beautiful countryside in Britain. They never forget Brathay. We get a very positive feedback from the students. Many of them return. And it's all important because a lot of these bright young people are going to be important and influential in their own countries in a few years' time.'

Alder told me about Brathay's work in what is called Outdoor Management Development, and the theory behind the training. 'The work is based on Kolb's learning cycle: first there is the action or the experience, then comes a period of review and reflection on that experience in which you draw your conclusions. They you apply the lessons learned to your next experience, and so the cyclical process continues. It is sometimes simplified into three imperatives: do, review and apply. According to the theory, those who follow the cycle conscientiously will continuously improve their performance.'

Alder says she can usually tell quite early on which of her groups are going to get real long-term benefits from the course. 'Some groups are clearly enjoying themselves but in a light-hearted way, and you know that when they get back to their jobs they will probably forget what they have learned, and revert to their old ways Other groups, while enjoying the challenges and experiences just as much, are also beginning to see the point of all the analysis and discussion. You feel sure that they will go on applying the Brathay methods in their working life, continuously improving their effectiveness, putting more into their work and getting more out of it.'

Three other courses were running on the Brathay campus at the same time as that large Manchester Business School course: a three-day course on Developing Leadership Skills for staff from BBC Resources North, a seven-day course to prepare 17 young people from the Royal Navy and Royal Marines (five of them women) for their appearance before the Admiralty Interview Board in the hope of moving on to officer training, and 20 sixth-formers from Merchiston Castle School doing a five-day course called Providing Opportunities for Change, which dealt with self-confidence, teamwork, taking responsibility as leaders and showing initiative. Brathay was now very busy, working almost to full capacity.

INVESTORS IN PEOPLE

For the past three years Brathay has been working towards obtaining the prestigious Investors in People award, a recognition of having reached certain standards in staff training and development. Brathay is one of the first outdoor training providers to qualify for this award. On 1 March, 1996, Lord Whitelaw visited Brathay to make the presentation, a fitting climax to Brathay's recent recovery and success.

The occasion was a double celebration because, as a perfect testimony to the value of Brathay training, the international truck and bus manufacturers Scania (GB) Ltd also had a present to give. Brathay provides the first and last modules of the firm's staff development programme and had thus helped over 150 of the company's employees in the past four years. Graham Cramp of Scania commented:

Brathay's contribution is vital to the success of our training scheme. They provide a disparate group of staff with a common focus, bond them together as a team and motivate them to succeed on the intense course that culminates in a Certificate in Management Studies from Leicester University.

Scania claimed that it was its experiences on Brathay courses that had enabled it to win the National Training Award in its sphere. Not only did Scania want to thank Brathay publicly for its share in that success, it had had made a replica of that handsome award to present to Brathay because Brathay had helped to make it all possible.

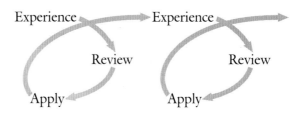

THEME 10:
THE BRATHAY ACHIEVEMENT

THE TURBULENT RIVER

Brathay is a turbulent place. It always has been. Anywhere that generates ideas and tries to put them into practice is likely to be volatile. But turbulence, handled properly, can be creative.

There is a river in Iceland that has sources in two very different types of terrain. One is in a pleasant open valley and the water flows down pure and clear. The other source is a glacier, and the water that spews out from beneath this erosive giant is a dirty brown. The scene where these two tributaries meet is dramatic. For a while they flow side by side, each maintaining its own integrity. Then, with much turbulence, they mix. The result is a rather uninteresting-looking compromise, yet, within that compromise, the river has gained resources far richer than before. Within all that 'dirt' from the glacier lie the nutrients and the building blocks for the lowlands and the landscapes yet to be formed.

In founding Brathay, Francis Scott wanted to enable new ideas to flow into the stream of educational thought. He provided the channel through which these ideas could flow. And, as we have seen, for 50 years a succession of people have poured their ideas and skills along this channel. Sometimes those ideas have only flowed for a short time, like Holidays with Purpose or the help for convalescent youngsters, but they served to pave the way for other, better ideas that followed in their wake. Some ideas have just dried up, like the once very active Field Study Centre, while others, such as Brathay's work with the Manpower Services Commission (MSC), have been 'taken on the flood and ridden', and then Brathay has returned to calmer waters.

The meeting of ideas

The stream of Brathay work has not flowed in isolation. Like those Icelandic streams, sooner or later Brathay had to meet the mainstream of education and training. Other people's ideas may be different from Brathay's, and when they meet the confluence can be turbulent. Perhaps the most fundamental difference is in the way the Brathay staff look at people. People are individuals with strengths and weaknesses. The role of Brathay is to seek out their talents and apply them to best use, whereas the mainstream approach has conventionally been to see people as vessels that need to be filled up with knowledge and skills. This is a gross oversimplification, but it does point to the difficulty Brathay has so often had in showing outsiders what its work is really about.

One example of how the two approaches differ is in recent concerns over safety in the outdoors. In the newsletter of the National Association for Outdoor Education, Dr Bertie Everard recalls that some years ago safety concerns in his firm, ICI, were met by more and more regulations. But safety did not improve. It was only when the problem was approached by applying what we now call development training, which invited people not just to obey the rules, but to study the problem as they saw it, to come up with more positive ways of working and to value safety more highly, that safety improved. This approach is fundamental to Brathay courses.

The spread of the Brathay message

In fact much of the experience of Brathay has flowed into the mainstream of the nation's life and education despite these difficulties. Brathay has also had influence abroad, as Brian Ware found in Australia. The founder of a successful outdoor centre in Africa in the 1960s went out of his way last year to say how much he owed to the inspiration of Brathay and its approach. In 50 years, almost 100,000 people have passed through one or other of its courses. Many of them have spoken of the effect Brathay had on them and their attitude to life, work and other people.

Brathay's influence has not only been through its users. Some 800 staff have passed through Brathay in 50 years taking the spirit and the style of the place with them. Publications by former staff spread the Brathay message. The most notable of these is probably Roger Greenaway's paper *The Competences of Development Trainers*, which has become a standard work. In the wider field he has produced *Playback: A Guide To Reviewing Activities* for the Duke of Edinburgh's Award, and the handbook *More Than Activities* for Save the Children and Endeavour Scotland, both of which acknowledge Brathay as a principal source. (Recent other publications about work at Brathay are listed in Appendix F.)

One of the privileges – and penalties – of being a pioneer is that others will copy, and maybe even improve, your product. Although Brathay has been modest about publicising its work, others have not been slow to notice it and to use it in their own work. Brathay, too, has learned a lot from others. Barrels and planks are not new; this author remembers some remarkably similar exercises with teams having to cross hypothetical ravines and 'electric' fences on the Army officer selection courses in the late 1940s. But for every idea passed on, a new one has been invented. Brathay's particular ability has been to create and adapt ideas, and so improve the effectiveness of outdoor management development.

BRATHAY AND MAINSTREAM EDUCATION

Brathay is once again focusing its attention on pupils in mainstream education and it is interesting to observe Brathay's stance, now and in the past, in relation to education and training. First there is the issue of the interface between the course members coming from schools and those coming from industry. Scott would have been aware that it was considered valuable to mix the two during the 1930s and 1940s. At Brathay the interface first became a reality in the Brathay Exploration Group (BEG) with its conscious division of places between the two sectors. Leaders saw that everyone had useful skills to offer, some intellectual, some mechanical, some just pure good sense. In such thinking the BEG was way ahead of its time.

The Oxfordshire schools courses in the 1950s gave Brathay its first chance to team up with conventional school staff. No research was ever done to quantify the extent to which their 'discovery' methods changed the lives of the staff and pupils, but it is a fact that, in the years immediately following that pioneering work, the whole outdoor centre movement in the UK took off.

Management training.

Equally significant must be the influence of the Brathay Field Study Centre. When it began there was no national Field Study Centre in the Lake District, and its immediate success must be attributed to the fact that, thanks to the generosity of various trusts, it was able to provide high quality courses of a kind directly related to the needs of sixth-formers and those on university courses. Over 25,000 young people benefited from the courses and the residential experience. Although this work did not evolve into a development training experience (in the usual sense), it left a strong mark on many people (see Theme 4).

For many years the Ministry of Education had, among its duties, a watching brief on the use of the outdoors in education. There was an Outdoor Education Advisory Committee, on which Brathay had been represented from its earliest days. Its members included inspectors of education and this author representing the BEG. A number of the committee's annual courses for teachers were held at Brathay, whose staff made a significant input. At the 1980 conference at Brathay, this thinking was taken forward by not only talking about the Adair model, but actually involving all the conference members in action-centred leadership throughout their stay. Those who attended went home changed.

Personal and social education

Brathay is following a different route from that of field studies in its return to working with schools. This time Brathay is working with schools that have decided to use the outdoors in their fulfilment of the national curriculum requirements for personal and social education (PSE). One example of this, the Garstang Youth Project, is described in the first chapter. However, such work is only possible if it is subsidised. At Brathay that subsidy takes two forms: financial, some of which comes from Brathay's own funds, and the assistance provided by the school staff, who share the duties and contribute to running of the course.

THE OUTDOOR ELEMENT

However Brathay expands, contracts or changes its courses, there is always one constant in the mix: the Lake District itself. Scott wanted youth training to take place within 'ideal surroundings provided by nature'. The extent to which Brathay courses can make use of that environment depends upon how much clients appreciate its value as a training ground. With shorter courses and the need to target defined objectives, there are fewer opportunities to use it than there were in the days of the four-week courses. Nevertheless, while Brathay itself may have of necessity to turn away from the hills with some of its courses, the realisation of the value of the outdoors is reflected in the growth in the number of outdoor centres: there were just 24 in 1962 rising to a peak of 1200 in 1981.

BRATHAY AND MANAGEMENT TRAINING

Brathay moved into the management training field because of its success in the personal development of young people. The experiment showed that this worked equally well with young leaders and senior managers. However, this work has been successful because of a very strong emphasis on quality and flexibility in response to a constantly changing market. The proof of this is that so many customers still prefer to use Brathay despite the fact that the field is now awash with competitors, many of whom offer cheaper courses.

A survey carried out by the Association for Management Education and Development (AMED) in 1991, *Developing the Developers*, lists a whole range of priorities for management training. These confirm the value of Brathay's focus and learning methods in leadership, team building and organisation development. Courses with too much emphasis on the outdoors are less favoured now, so Brathay's traditional balance between physical and creative work is highly relevant. The bulk of management development training occurs in companies, colleges, and the business schools. Brathay has a particular experience to offer and this is now much used by, for example, the business schools of the universities of Durham and Manchester.

Brathay's management work is now taking on an international dimension. One recent course was carried out in Russian for a group of businessmen from the former Soviet Union, and many courses are now conducted away from Brathay at clients' requests. For example, two of the training staff recently ran a course in Antwerp for a multinational.

Regular appreciation events are held at Brathay, at which potential clients can test the facilities and methods used on the course. Much emphasis is now placed on evaluation, and there is increasing use of up to date academic techniques to achieve this. A summary of this work was published in Brathay's spring newsletter.

BRATHAY AND SPECIAL NEEDS

It takes a special kind of devotion to work successfully with many of the youngsters who come on Brathay courses. Over the years there has been no shortage of people willing to take on that sometimes very difficult work.

Brathay's contribution to the training of people with special needs lies not in any esoteric skills, but rather in using the same techniques that are applied so successfully on all its courses: patience, care (love, if you like) and imagination. Whatever their station in life, their fortune or misfortune, people will listen if you show that you care for them and are prepared to take them and their hopes and fears seriously.

Imagination is the key to all Brathay's work, whether it be a complex management exercise or getting all the kids at Eagle Crag to write themselves a letter on the last day about their own feelings on the course. The tutor keeps the letters, and posts them off to them precisely three months later.

ONE OFF OR LONG TERM?

Originally it was thought that a one-off residential experience could be so influential and so beneficial that it could stand alone. 'Old Boys' returning decades later in 1996 testify to its value. But even in the earliest days there was a current of feeling that this was not enough. A suggestion was made that such a residential period might prove especially beneficial if preparations for it were made in the firm or school beforehand and if similar action were taken afterwards.

It took over 20 years for this concept to take root, because in order to implement it, not only the training centre but also its clients have to be persuaded of the value of the before and after process. Brathay was among the first to develop this process, which is now a normal part of its approach.

COMMUNICATION AND VALUES

Brathay's staff spend much of their time seeking to understand the needs of others and to respond to these through the course programmes. One of the ironies of being in this work is that staff can lose sight of the very thing they are helping others to learn. Brathay has, at times, become confused about what it stands for. Tensions have existed and communication has not always been good. The corporate effort 15 years ago to draw up the Brathay philosophy did much to bring people together. Recently, staff quite spontaneously worked out an agreed statement of values, something in which all staff – training, marketing, administrative and domestic – were involved (see Appendix B). All staff now regularly meet at process reviews to consider ways of improving things as part of a programme to make a good Brathay become even better.

THE BROAD RIVER

If Brathay's history has demonstrated anything it is that it will always be remembered for its warm welcome, its personal contacts, and the way it received and treated its clients. Perhaps for the first time in their lives, what they said and did seemed to matter; other people's safety and welfare depended upon their actions. All this adds up to a formula which, however much it is associated with an old building in a wonderful setting in the Lake District, can be applied – by the right people – anywhere. It is infinitely extendible.

When he first bought Brathay Hall, Francis Scott was honest enough to admit that he had little idea what he would use it for. He just wanted to preserve the place and its setting. But, like a trainer on a Brathay course, he was ready for the ideas to flow in. He was ready to use the best, directing that best into a hundred useful channels. The 'turbulence' that may be caused by that flow of ideas is a necessary part of any new development. Out of this pioneer work has come a tide of benefit for individuals, organisations and communities, broader in many ways than even Francis Scott could have envisaged.

EPILOGUE

Brian Liversidge was determined to make Brathay's 50th anniversary a year to remember, and, indeed, 1996 has been well and truly marked (on top of a full programme of normal work). Brathay's public profile is already much enhanced.

A painting was commissioned from Julian Heaton-Cooper, a well known Lake District artist. The original now hangs in the Hall, and has been reproduced as the cover of this book and as a very saleable postcard.

This history, telling as it does the Brathay story against a background of changes in training and education, itself makes a key contribution to the celebration of 50 years of progress.

But most importantly, the work itself goes forward. Over four memorable days in July, the Brathay campus was host to a youth conference of 200 people, to a challenge event when companies fielded teams to compete against each other, to a reunion of former course members and staff, and to a public open day.

That youth conference, entitled 'Development Training Beyond 2000', was chaired by Sir Christopher Ball, director of learning of the Royal Society of Arts. It was attended by professionals in education, in training, and in youth and social work. They addressed the issues in these fields, discussed examples of good practice in the UK and from overseas, and developed ideas for future action. In his summary, Ball particularly highlighted the need to underpin development training with a satisfactory theoretical base and to provide better research evidence of its effectiveness. He challenged Brathay to take the work of that conference forward. The young people who experience development training now are a tiny proportion of those who could benefit from it. There is a vital national need to take this way of learning to a far wider audience, and all those involved in the work have a mountain still to climb.

In September, just as this book is being published, Brathay will spotlight its work with managers with another major conference, this time chaired by Professor John Adair. There is a strong team of speakers including Edward de Bono, Meredith Belbin and Tudor Rickards, Those names, and Brathay's standing, have in turn pulled in the delegates. Under the title 'Pioneers of Change', they will debate how individuals, teams and technology, as well as organisations themselves, actually achieve change.

This is a conference where thinkers and doers come together. They will thrash out what works and what doesn't, and they will argue and explore how best to handle that demand and need for change that is an inescapable part of modern life. Appropriately, in line with Brathay's fundamental aim, the financial surplus from this conference will directly fund future youth work.

Both these conferences help to set a new agenda and widen horizons for Brathay. As this small, independent, but remarkably influential Trust embarks on another 50 years of progress, there is still so much to do.

Mark Wolfson

APPENDIX A:
FIFTY YEARS OF GROWTH

1946   Foundation of Brathay Hall Centre.
            Dick Faithfull-Davies, warden.

1947   Holidays with Purpose courses.
            Start of Brathay Exploration Group (BEG).
            Surveys of Easedale and Angle tarns.

1949   Hall accommodation expanded to take 47 boys (from 24).

1950   J.B. Macmillan, warden.
            Four-week courses begin.
            First BEG overseas expedition (Norway).

1951   Old Brathay becomes available. Uses include Holidays with Purpose.
            First BEG New Year leaders' meeting.

1952   Establishment of BEG base in huts in the woods.

1953   J.E. Thompson, warden.
            BEG Iceland Expedition.
            Warden's house (Brathay Knott).

1954   J.F.M. Doogan, warden.
            Staff common room cabin.

1955   Oxfordshire School courses begin.
            Boathouse for five whalers and five dinghies.

1956   Nine four-week courses a year becomes the norm.
            Dormitory block on site of Old Brathay greenhouse.
            First BEG Foula expedition.

1959   Oxfordshire courses move to Patterdale.
            Old Brathay converted into conference centre.

1960   Theatre block.
            H.M. Inspectors' report.

1961   Second dormitory block in grounds above the first.

1962   G.M. Wolfson, warden.
            BEG expedition to Uganda.
            'Follow-up' courses

1964   New dormitory block for BEG.

1965   Junior courses begin (usually two a year).
        Documentary film: *Brathay Hall Centre*.
        Two staff houses in woods.

1966   A.J.C. Cochrane, warden.
        Extensions to Old Brathay (house: Little Brathay).

1967   A.B. Ware, principal.
        Brathay Field Study Centre, M.A.E. Mortimer, director.
        Francis Scott Laboratory.

1968   C. Rose, bursar/administrative officer.
        Hall dormitories fitted with bunks.

1969   Responsibility at Work courses, with Industrial Society.
        Courses for trainee managers.
        Conversion of lower dormitories for Field Study use.
        A.E. Land, secretary of BEG.
        Low Brathay (principal's house).
        First mixed courses at the Hall.

1970   D.H. Freeman, warden.
        New BEG kitchen/common room and ablutions.
        Old Brathay dormitories fitted with bunks.
        Establishment of the John Doogan Library at the Field Study Centre.
        Mountain Leadership course.

1971   First Bulmers courses.
        New staff room and guest room block behind the Hall.
        L. Hayball, first female instructor.
        R.J. Metcalfe, secretary of BEG.
        Publication of *Handbook for Expeditions*.

1972   Courses for individual companies.
        Double dormitory on hill behind the Hall.
        Twenty-fifth anniversary of foundation.
        Publication of *Brathay – The First 25 Years* (Dr Bruce Campbell).

1973   Whitfield report on four-week courses.
        Managers in Action courses.
        Start of Trident courses.
        Friends of Brathay founded.

1974   Dining/kitchen block for Hall.
        (Bulmers set up Leadership Trust.)
        C.J. Folland, BEG secretary.

1975   C.H. Chambers, director of training.
        I.W. Swanson, director of marketing.
        John Lewis courses.
        Second Whitfield report.
        BEG has 363 members on expeditions.
        End of four-week courses.

1976   Delegate days (including BEG) peak at over 30,000.
        Intermediate Treatment courses.

1977   Hall work renamed Brathay Training Opportunities.
        Foundation of Development Training Advisory Group (DTAG).

1978   Old Brathay becomes Centre for Exploration and Field Studies.
        Conversion of barn to give accommodation and meeting room
        (job creation project).
        Conversion of second hut into laboratory (giving four in all).
        A. Brown, director of training.
        C. Clephan, BEG co-ordinator.
        New edition of *Expedition Handbook*.
        Proposal to build John Lewis Centre abandoned.

1979   Death of F.C. Scott, aged 97.
        M.H. Gee, head of Centre for Exploration and Field Studies.
        Theatre block extended to give six group rooms.
        Establishment of Tiny Wyke as follow-up base for groups.

1980   MSC Youth Opportunities Programme.
        Delegate days at Field Study Centre peak at over 12,000.
        Two staff houses built in walled garden.

1981   M. Housden, head of Centre for Leadership and Development Training.
        Eagle Crag Intermediate Treatment (IT) centre.
        Friends of Brathay revived.
        Music room becomes bar/common room.
        The Marsh report, includes Brathay philosophy and purpose.

1982   D. Spragg, development officer.
        Achievement of RSA Education for Capability award.
        Refurbishing of Hall dormitories with better bunks.
        Acland report.
        Acquisition of Portacabin for administration of MSC work.
        First Francis Scott Memorial Lecture (on Intermediate Treatment).
        Merger of administration – the two-centre concept is no longer relevant.
        'Activity areas' introduced:
            1. Development Training for Industry/Commerce (S. Crowther).
            2. Environmental Studies (M. Mortimer).
            3. IT at Eagle Crag (L. Partridge).
            4. YTS for Unemployed (S. Valentine).
            5. Training the Trainers (D. Spragg).
            6. BEG.

1983   Brathay–Rank Knowsley Urban Leadership project.
        Death of M. Mortimer.
        D. Richards, principal of Brathay.
        New BEG leaders' bunkroom (job creation project).

1984   Brathay becomes MSC accredited training centre.
        Additional offices between Hall and dining room.
        Old Brathay with Eagle Crag named Centre for Youth Learning.

1985   Salford Urban Leadership project.
         S. Dickinson, BEG officer.
         Fund raising campaign raises £750,000.

1986   Cessation of Field Study courses.
         MSC Rural Enterprise Project.
         Eagle Crag extended.
         BEG Development Study.
         Site accommodation: 181 beds overall (including guests/visiting staff).

1987   Mainstream delegate days peak at over 14,000.
         Progressive withdrawal of Scott Trust subvention.

1988   Separation of trustee and governing bodies.
         Provision of mobile trailer unit for off-site work.
         BEG 40th anniversary celebration at Royal Geographical Society.

1989   J. Manifold, chief executive.
         BEG becomes independent.
         Conversion of top dormitory into 12 single *en suite* Loughrigg Rooms.

1990   Last year of Scott subvention.
         Recession closes ATC scheme.
         D. Davies, services manager.

1991   Council of trustees.
         I. Swanson, acting chief executive.
         A. Cowl, finance officer.
         Old Brathay let to Charlotte Mason College (for three years).

1992   B. Liversidge, chief executive.
         The Five-Year Plan.

1993   S. Lenartowicz, head of youth department.

1994   Virtual doubling of youth numbers in a year.
         Wansfell Rooms become *en suite*.

1995   Youth numbers on a par with adult numbers.
         Record number on BEG overseas expeditions.
         Refurbishing of Old Brathay kitchen and dining room.
         Achievement of Investors in People award.

1996   Refurbishment of Old Brathay dormitories and group rooms.
         Overall capacity restored to 120+ beds.
         Conversion of Hall top floor to *en suite* rooms.
         Fiftieth anniversary celebrations:
             1. Francis C. Scott Memorial Lecture given at Royal Society of Arts
                by Trevor Phillips.
             2. 'Development Training Beyond 2000' youth conference.
             3. 'Pioneers of Change' management development symposium.
             4. Alumni reunion.

APPENDIX B:
THE BRATHAY HALL TRUST:
ITS PHILOSOPHY AND PURPOSE

The Brathay Hall Trust was founded by Francis Scott in 1946. Its main aim, in his words, was:

...the opening of young people's minds to the possibilities of living adventurously in the world of physical activity as well as in the world of the spirit.

The central purpose of the Trust is to promote all-round development of young people. The Trust seeks to achieve this purpose in four ways.

1. By offering young people the opportunity to live for a short time in a community on 'safe' ground away from home, school, or work environment. The atmosphere is informal, friendly and supportive and is sustained by the personal example and dedication of the staff.

2. By utilising the superb natural setting and facilities of Brathay to challenge and stretch young people both physically and mentally in a variety of situations designed to promote and accelerate their development and learning through self-discovery.

3. By helping young people to analyse their performance and achievements both as individuals and as group members and thereby to increase their understanding and care for others, and to relate their experience at Brathay to their lives at work and at home.

4. By helping those who influence young people – managers, teachers and others – to understand more about the potential of those for whom they are responsible.

The following objectives apply to development training courses, but they also form an essential background to the more specific educational aims of the field study courses and to Brathay expeditions.

People coming to Brathay are encouraged to:

-   develop their resourcefulness and capability
-   widen their horizons, broaden their experience and extend their capacity
    for enjoyment
-   gain self-confidence and self-awareness combined with humility
-   form and develop true values and perspectives with opportunity for reflection
-   work together effectively in small groups, developing a sensitivity to the views and
    aspirations of others and the ability to form constructive and sympathetic relationships
-   develop the use of initiative and the ability to identify and solve problems,
    and to make responsible decisions about life and work
-   develop creativity and communications skills
-   explore their own potential, motivation and ambition
-   develop an appreciation and understanding of the natural environment,
    and a recognition of man's place within it and influence upon it
-   improve their ability to cope with change
-   set for themselves and strive to achieve the highest standards of which
    they are capable
-   relate their experience at Brathay to their home, school, work and leisure situations.

BRATHAY VALUES

The following statement of values was prepared by Brathay staff in 1994 in consultation with their colleagues and the trustees.

Mission:	**To excel in development training and so facilitate our commitment to young people.**
People:	**People are the reason for our existence and our most important resource.** Developing people is our business: we seek to practise what we preach. We aim to provide equality of opportunity. We value the physical and emotional safety of our customers and staff.
Teamwork:	**We value everyone's contribution to our success.** We value commitment, trust, integrity, openness and respect. We expect to give and receive support and loyalty. We strive to communicate effectively, and particularly value listening.
Quality:	**We value excellence in all we do.** We express pride in our mission and our history. We endeavour to provide excellent service to our customers. We encourage and celebrate success. We strive for continuous improvement.
Environment:	**We value the environment within which we work.** We wish to ensure that our actions conserve the beauty of the estate and of the Lake District. We aspire to making our impact on the global environment sustainable.

APPENDIX C:
CATALOGUE OF COURSES
AND SUMMARY OF STATISTICS

1. **Holidays with Purpose**
    Multi-activity weeks for boys aged 15–18 years inclusive. 'Providing boys from industry with enjoyable holidays of an unusual character.' Started in 1947. Continued (later in Old Brathay) until 1955.

2. **Winter Convalescent breaks**
    Duration one to two weeks. Started winter 1947. Continued until 1951.

3. **Brathay Exploration Group**
    From 1947. Usually between 12 and 20 expeditions a year.
    (For full details see Appendix D.)

4. **The standard four-week courses**
    Residential courses for boys in industry using the activities already featured in Holidays with Purpose: fellcraft, lakecraft, workshop, arts, crafts, drama, and discussions. For boys aged 16–19 years. Mixed courses from 1969.
    Began 1950. Continued until 1975.

5. **Oxfordshire school courses**
    Six-week courses for 24 Secondary Modern schoolboys in their last year (age 14), part-staffed by their masters (three) and part by Brathay. Based at Old Brathay.
    From 1955 to 1958.
    Course devised with Brathay Hall staff with elements as in standard courses plus basic school/field studies.

6. **Chivers girls' courses**
    Originated in links Brian Ware made when tutor at Impington Village College.
    One-week courses held between main courses. One a year. From 1952 to 1959.

7. **British Council courses**
    Walks and cultural talks for internationally mixed adult groups. Usually based at Old Brathay. From 1955 to 1958.

8. **Conferences at Old Brathay**
    Old Brathay with 18 beds. From 1959 to 1962.

9. **Follow-up courses**
    (a) 'Brathay Two'. Initially at Brathay then climbing in Glencoe.
         Offered sailing, art, drama. From 1962 to 1965.
    (b) John Lewis returners. 1977 only.
    (c) Opportunities to come back on (self-planned) weeks at Tiny Wyke (the restored boathouse cottage) holding 10. Also camping (maximum six) on the boathouse headland. From 1977 to 1984.
    (d) 'Brathay Beyond'. Two one-week courses in August 1986 at Old Brathay.

10. **Junior courses**
     Content devised by Sir Percy Lord, chief education officer for Lancashire.
     1965–70: Two courses a year of 26 days each. Mostly boys from Lancashire.
     1971–76: Between one and four 14-day courses. Mixed from 1973.
     1977–78: 'Preparing for Work'. Three courses of 11 days each.

11. **Field Study Centre courses**
     The Centre was opened in 1967 and 'grew out of the experience of the Exploration Group
     in pioneering adventurous field studies'. Based at Old Brathay with accommodation for 24
     students and six visiting staff.
     Courses were offered for sixth-form students in A-level geography and biology. The centre
     was also available to universities and teacher training colleges to run their own courses.
     All courses ran for seven days, Wednesday to Wednesday.
     1974: plans to run annual summer school every August.
     1977: centre reorganised as Centre for Exploration and Field Studies.
     Aim: 'to consider the whole range of field studies both on Field Study Centre courses and
     on Exploration Group expeditions'.
     1986: cessation of field study courses.

12. **Responsibility at Work courses**
     'For young men aged 18–21 years to relate the experience of leadership, responsibility and
     teamwork on the mountains and of creative opportunity, to greater effectiveness at work'.
     14 days. Run jointly with the Industrial Society. Included all the normal Brathay activities
     except sailing.
     1969: one course.
     1970–72: Four or five courses a year.
     1970–71: special eight-day courses for trainee managers.
     1973–76: these developed into 'Leadership for Managers', 'Managers in Action', and
     'Preparing for Leadership'.

13. **Mountain Leadership courses**
     Introductory and Assessment. Mixed courses open to general public. Seven days.
     1970–76: one course a year. Held at Old Brathay.

14. **Bulmers courses**
     'The basis of this course is the belief that the leadership training given by Brathay to youth
     in industry and commerce over the past 25 years should be extended into the management
     field.'
     Sometimes described as Brathay Management Course.
     1971–73: two courses a year for all ages; 24 – 36 on a course. 10 days.
     1979: one further Bulmer course.

15. **Customised courses**
     Courses for individual firms based on Bulmer and 'Responsibility at Work' experience.
     From 1972: initially three or four a year. Firms catered for: GEC, John Lewis Partnership,
     Marks & Spencer, Post Office, Caterpillar Ltd, RTZ Corporation, Chemical & Allied
     Products Training Board, Newcastle University.
     Also football apprentices, Unified Vocational Preparation (UVP): two six day courses for
     shoe industry.
     Trainees weekend for Silentnight, graduate course. (Eight days for 25 people)
     Executive weekend: 'to let executives of Securicor experience Brathay first hand so as to
     support trainees who had been to Brathay'.

16.   **Trident Trust courses**
      Part of a three-pronged government scheme to help young people (especially those from
      high unemployment areas) in their transition from school to work. 10 days at BEG huts.
      1973–1990: Up to four courses a year.
      Some Trident people also took part in BEG lakes expeditions.

17.   **Intermediate Treatment (IT) courses**
      'Schemes aimed to reduce delinquency by involving young people in constructive
      activities.'
      1976: Using BEG huts as base, 21 group visits involving 58 children from St Helens
      (5+2+2+2 days each).
      1977–80: Similar numbers.
      1981 onwards: based on the new IT centre at Eagle Crag.
      Other authorities also involved.
      Ends 1983.

18.   **Brathay Training Opportunities**
      A blanket name for all programmed industrial/commercial courses, comprising:
      1977: (a) 'Responsibility at Work'. Two courses.
                  (See 12 above. Now 19 days.)
             (b) 'Preparing for Leadership'. Four courses.
                  A 14-day course 'for young men/women age 18–25 years about to be
                  responsible for the work of others or already in junior supervisory
                  positions'.
             (c) 'Managers in Action'. Two courses.
                  A nine-day course 'for men/women up to age 50'.
             (d) Special courses tailored for individual firms based on (a), (b) and (c).
      1978: Dispositions: (a) 15% (b) 35% (c) 4.5% (d) 45%.
             Ages: 95% of Brathay Training Opportunities and 98% overall were under 25
             years.
      1980: Add: (e) 'Supervising for Results'. One 10-day course 'for men/women with
             current responsibility for direct supervision'.
             Courses began to shift away from traditional involvement with the broad range of
             young people and move up market into the management/leadership field. An
             emphasis on a wide mix of largely customised courses for people of all ages in
             work. Companies found: 'Brathay's distinctive brand of development training a
             good basis for staff development in conjunction with their own in-house training'
             (annual report). Some courses held away from Brathay.

      1981: Summary:
                  (A) Thirteen open courses with 383 delegates.
                  (B) Eighteen company courses with 537 delegates. (See 19.)
      1983: Courses offered include:
                  (a) 'Leadership in Action'. Six courses. Six days.
                  (b) 'Supervisors in Action'. Three courses. Six days.
                  (c) 'Managers in Action'. Three courses. Six days.
                  (d) 'Preparing for Leadership'. Three courses. 12 days.
                  (e) 'Responsibility at Work'. Two courses. 14 days.
                  (f) 'Team Building'. Three courses. Four days.
                  (g) Various courses for trainers and tutors. Nine courses.
                      Two to 11 days.

19. **The youth programme**
Working in parallel with 18 '...to give a more co-ordinated response to the development needs of young people'.

 1981: Summary:
     (C) 23 UVP/YOP/IT/Trident courses with 282 delegates. (UVP and YOP were run in response to the government's new training initiatives/Manpower Services Commission (MSC) Unemployment proposals.)
     (D) One disabled people's course.
 1983: The YTS and Youth Development Programme 'to provide learning opportunities from which young people can discover potential and so make realistic plans for improving both the quality of their lives and the contribution which they make to society'. Based partly at Old Brathay but mostly at Eagle Crag.
   Work includes:
   (a) 1983–86: Knowsley and Salford urban leadership projects: 'to identify and train young people with potential for leadership and voluntary service in their community'. At Brathay and elsewhere.
   (b) 1986–90: Rural enterprise: to help long-term unemployed in Cumbria develop their skills and so move into self-employment, education or jobs'.
   (c) 1988: Three disabled people's courses.

20. **Accredited training centre**
1984–90: a 'Training the Trainers' scheme set up for the MSC 'to provide development opportunities for trainers of young people'. Run partly on-site and partly elsewhere. Brathay was the accredited training centre for Cumbria and the north-west.

21. **The five-year plan 1992–96**
Re-establishes prime purposes of Brathay:
1. To provide young people with experiences that encourage their physical, moral and intellectual development.
2. To investigate and research into questions affecting this education process.
3. To train people concerned with the development of young people.

 1992: Vigorous expansion of a wide range of (mainly customised) management courses at the Hall.
 1993: Re-establishment of youth work at Eagle Crag base with courses for all levels and needs of youth.
 1995: Old Brathay and barn re-open for youth and management courses.
   Second five-year plan. Total number of courses: 322, comprising 122 youth and 200 management development.
   Over 90% of the current courses, in both youth work and management development are designed to the requirements of the client. It is therefore not possible to produce a summary list for the later years.
 1996: public courses:
   (a) 'Managers in Action'. Three courses. Seven days.
   (b) 'Leadership in Action'. Two courses. Seven days.
   (c) 'Preparing for Leadership'. One course. Seven days.
   (d) 'Personal Development'. Three courses. Five days.
   (e) 'Personal Development for Professionals'. Two courses. Five days.
   (f) 'Graduate Development' (appreciation event). One course. Two days.

NUMBERS ATTENDING COURSES: SUMMARY OF STATISTICS

Delegate days

A delegate day is defined as one day attended by one delegate/trainee/student.
The estimated grand total of delegate days is 804,303.

Age spread

Prior to 1984 under 25s accounted for about 90% of the total, and prior to 1976, virtually 100%.
Over the 49 years, 88% of the totals have been for people aged under 25.
The 1995 age spread was 55% under 25.

Totals

In overall delegate days, the relative sizes of each of the main Brathay operations appears to have been: Field Study Centre, 22%; Brathay Exploration Group, 15%; mainstream and other Hall activities, 63%.

During the 19 years of its operation (1967 to 1986), the Field Study Centre was 40% of the whole operation and the Field Study Centre plus BEG totalled 54% of the delegate days. In all the field study years, except the first two and the last three, the delegate day totals, plus those of BEG, exceeded those of the main 'Hall' courses.

Course length and number of delegates

Hall course lengths have changed from the 28 days for standard courses in the 1950s and 1960s, to a current average of 3.5 days for youth and 2.2 days for management development courses. Hence the numbers now going through are the highest ever.

In 1994 there were 4064 delegates, and 4577 in 1995. For comparison with 1958 (which had a similar delegate day total) the number of individuals going through in a year was only about 700.

In the first 25 years there were around 14,000 delegates.

In the second 25 years there were more than 80,000, making a grand total of more than 90,000.

Course type

The other big change over the years has been in course type.
Whereas in the 1950s the Hall was running one standard open course, now in any one year there are over 300 specially tailored courses, and 12 or more open courses.

APPENDIX D:
BRATHAY EXPLORATION GROUP EXPEDITIONS:
A COMPLETE CATALOGUE

1947   The first expeditions (two tarn surveys) took part within Holidays with Purpose.

1948   Expedition to Blea Water, 16 boys for 10 days.

1949   Group formally established but Hall-based.
Four Lake District expeditions.

1950   Four Lake District expeditions.
Geographical survey expedition to Norway.

1951   First New Year leaders' meeting, annual thereafter.
Four Lake District expeditions.
Lakes courses designed as training for those later going on overseas expeditions.

1952   Establishment of HQ in the woods, 16 + 4 beds
BEG council.
Four Lake District expeditions.
One Norway expedition.

1953   Four Lake District expeditions.
Expeditions to Norway and Iceland.

1954   Four Lake District expeditions.
Expeditions to Norway and Yugoslavia.

1955   Six Lake District expeditions, including two at Easter.
Expeditions to Norway and Yugoslavia.

1956   Six Lake District expeditions.
Two expeditions to Foula and two to Norway.

1957   Six Lake District expeditions. Two expeditions to Foula and Snowdonia.
One each to Norway and Iceland.

1958   Six Lake District expeditions. Two expeditions to Foula and Norway.
One each to Snowdonia, Yugoslavia and the Pyrenees.

1959   Six Lake District expeditions. Three expeditions to Foula.
One each to Snowdonia, Norway, Iceland and the Pyrenees.

1960   Six Lake District expeditions. Three expeditions to Foula.
One each to Norway, Yugoslavia and the Pyrenees.

1961   Six Lake District expeditions. Four expeditions to Foula.
One each to Iceland, Norway and Corsica.

1962   Six Lake District expeditions. Four expeditions to Foula.
        One each to Norway, Iceland, Tunisia and Uganda.

1963   Six Lake District expeditions. Four expeditions to Foula.
        Two expeditions to Iceland. One each to Norway Yugoslavia and Uganda.

1964   Six Lake District expeditions. Three expeditions to Foula.
        Two expeditions to Iceland. One each to Norway, Poland and Tunisia.

1965   Six Lake District expeditions. Four expeditions to Foula.
        Two expeditions to Iceland. One each to Ireland, Poland and Tunisia.

1966   Six Lake District expeditions. Three expeditions to Foula.
        One each to Ireland, the Faeroes, Iceland, Poland and Tunisia.

1967   Seven Lake District expeditions. Four expeditions to Foula.
        Two expeditions to Tunisia. One each to Ireland, Norway, Iceland and Greenland.

1968   Seven Lake District expeditions. Four expeditions to Foula.
        One each to Ireland, the Faeroes, Norway, Iceland, Tunisia and Kenya.

1969   Six Lake District expeditions. Four expeditions to Foula.
        Two to Iceland. One each to Greenland, Tunisia, the Cairngorms and the Monach
        Islands.

1970   Six Lake District expeditions. Four expeditions to Foula.
        One each to Inverpolly, the Faeroes, Iceland, Norway, Yugoslavia, Tunisia and Kenya.

1971   Six Lake District expeditions. Four expeditions to Foula.
        Two expeditions to Iceland. One each to Snowdonia, Inverpolly, St Kilda, Norway,
        Yugoslavia, Kenya and Turkey.

1972   Five Lake District expeditions. One leader training.
        Four expeditions to Foula. Two each to Iceland and Norway.
        One each to Greenland, Yugoslavia and the Scottish Highlands.

1973   Six Lake District expeditions. Five expeditions to Foula.
        Three to Iceland. One leader training. One each to Snowdonia, the Scottish Highlands,
        Norway and the Canaries.

1974   Six Lake District expeditions. One leader training.
        Five expeditions to Foula. Two each to Ireland and Norway.
        One each to Kenya, Gomera, the Scottish Highlands and Iceland.

1975   Six Lake District expeditions. One leader training.
        Four expeditions to Foula. Two each to the Scottish Highlands and Norway.
        One each to Ireland, Shetland, Iceland, Gomera and British Columbia (363 participants,
        including Canadian members).

1976   Five Lake District expeditions. Two leader training.
        Three expeditions to Scotland.
        One each to Staffa, Foula, Ireland, Iceland, Greenland, Norway, Ghana
        and the Canaries.

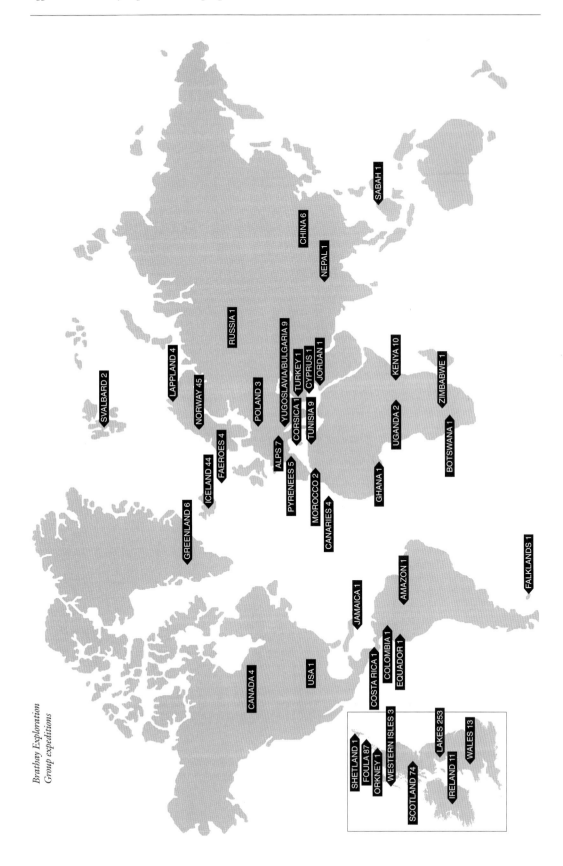

*Brathay Exploration
Group expeditions*

1977   BEG becomes part of Centre for Exploration and Field Studies.
       Five Lake District expeditions. One leader training.
       Four to Scotland, two to Iceland, and one each to Foula, Norway and Sabah.

1978   Five Lake District expeditions, some now training and called
       'Introduction to the Mountain Environment' (IME). One leader
       training. Five expeditions to Scotland, one each to Foula, Iceland, Norway and
       Lappland.

1979   Seven Lake District expeditions. One leader training.
       Four expeditions to Scotland, three to Iceland, two to Foula, one each to Norway, Kenya
       and the Canadian Rockies.

1980   Seven Lake District expeditions. Four to Scotland, two each to Foula
       and Iceland, and one each to the Faeroes, Norway, Kenya, and the Canadian Rockies.

1981   Seven Lake District expeditions. Six to Scotland, two to Foula, one
       each to Iceland, Kenya, Canadian Rockies and Costa Rica.

1982   Seven Lake District expeditions. Three to Scotland and one each
       to Ireland, the Faeroes, Iceland, Norway, Svalbard, Kenya, Equador and Foula.

1983   Seven Lake District expeditions. Four to Scotland, one each to Iceland, Greenland,
       Norway, Cyprus, Zimbabwe, Kenya and Jamaica.

1984   Eight Lake District expeditions. Five to Scotland, one each to Iceland,
       Lappland and Morocco.

1985   Five Lake District expeditions. Five to Scotland, one each to Wales, Norway, Svalbard,
       Greenland and Morocco.

1986   Five Lake District expeditions. One leader training.
       One each to the Pennines, Snowdonia, Pembrokeshire, Scotland, Iceland, China and the
       USA. First annual members' reunion.

1987   Four Lake District expeditions (including one special needs).
       Two leader training. Two expeditions to Norway, and one each to Snowdonia, Scotland
       and Iceland.

1988   Two Lake District expeditions. Two leader training.
       One each Scotland, the Alps, Norway, Jordan and China.

1989   One Lake District expedition. Two leader training. Two to Wales.
       One each to Scotland, the Alps, Iceland and the Falklands.

1990   Two Lake District expeditions. Three to Scotland. Two to Norway, one each to Orkney,
       Foula, the Pyrenees and China. 94 participants.

1991   One Lake District expedition. One leader training (Scotland).
       One each to Scotland, Snowdonia, Ireland, the Alps, Iceland and Botswana.

1992   One mountain first aid, one leader training. Two to Wales,
       one each to Scotland, the Alps, Norway, Lappland, Foula and China.

1993   One first aid, two leader training. Two expeditions to Scotland and
        one each to Foula, Spain, Norway and Colombia (the Amazon).

1994   One first aid and four leader training. One each to Foula, Scotland,
        Wales, the Alps, Norway, Iceland, Russia, Nepal and China. 198 participants.

1995   One first aid, three leader training. Two to the Alps and one each to
        Ireland, Norway, Lappland, Bulgaria, Kenya, the Amazon and China.

Total number of expeditions: 630

Total number of participants: 7884

Total number of leaders: 1796
(counting each attendance as a person)

APPENDIX E:
A BRATHAY FORTNIGHT

During a typical fortnight in June 1996, Brathay hosted the following courses.

Apprentices at Eagle Crag
Twenty young men and women from the Wolseley Group. Their 12-day programme represents real commitment by the company to staff development. Key themes include responsibility at work, developing self-confidence, team working and flexibility.

Garstang High School in the barn
A weekend for 20 students and four staff. This education partnership between Garstang High School, Lancashire, the Youth Service and Brathay, with mixed funding from statutory, charitable and local sources, helps to bring the personal and social education curriculum to life for Year 10 students (age 14).

Valuing cultural diversity, living in Old Brathay
The newly refurbished Old Brathay is hosting a group of 16 young first generation Anglo-Asian women from the old mill towns who are experiencing 'cultural confusion': at school they are bombarded with the pressures of Western culture, but at home they must maintain traditional values and behaviours. The four-day programme is designed to build their self-esteem, and to enable them to glimpse their true potential and make positive decisions about their future.

Trainer training in the Hall dormitories
A group of 10 Royal Air Force physical training instructors are on a one-week facilitation course, developing group skills and reviewing techniques to use on programmes at RAF Resource and Initiative Centres throughout the UK.

Rover Group in the Loughrigg Rooms
The process of 'learning by doing' lends itself well to team building/development; interesting projects, group working and critical review in a supportive environment. There are 16 participants on this four-day course.

Clearing bank in the Wansfell Rooms
Twenty-five newly-recruited staff from a new indirect banking centre came on a two-day team development programme, getting to know each other and learning to work together.

Executive leadership module in the local hotel
Living off-site but working on the estate, a group of nine senior managers from a paper manufacturing company spend four days rehearsing their strategic plans and refining interpersonal/departmental relationships.

APPENDIX F:
PUBLICATIONS

Brathay – The First 25 Years, Campbell, 1972
Associations of Clappersgate and Brathay, Storey, 1958
A Memoir of Francis Scott, Lewis, 1989
John Harden of Brathay Hall, Foskett, 1974
In Search of Adventure (the Hunt report), 1993
Personal Growth Through Adventure, Hopkins and Putnam, 1993
The Adventure Alternative, Mortlock, 1984
The History of Development Training, Everard, 1993

The Brathay Exploration Group has published a large number of reports including:

- Annual reports since 1956
- Annual accounts of expeditions 1952–71
- *Prayers for Use on Expeditions* (ed. Seaton), 1965
- *Expedition Handbook,* 2nd edn (ed. Land), Butterworths, 1978
- *Expedition Medicine,* 2nd edn (ed. Illingworth), Blackwell, 1984
- Over 80 reports on single expeditions or special surveys
- At least 72 BEG reports in other publications
- An index to all BEG publications up to 1986 is published by the Young Explorers' Trust

Between 1957 and 1976 16mm sound colour films were produced on the following (now available in video):

Lake District (tarn survey), Norway (glaciology),
Foula (ornithology), Iceland (expedition planning),
Uganda (partnerships), British Columbia (wilderness survey),
Greenland (archaeology), Brathay Hall (four-week course in 1965)

The Power to Change, video of management course, 1986

RECENT MANAGEMENT TRAINING REPORTS

'The changing vision of the outdoors', Ann Alder in *Management Training,* February 1995
'OMD: value for money, or a bit of a lark?', Phil Donnison in *Works Management,* April 1995
'Off on a works outing', Nicola Venning in the *Guardian,* 15th July, 1995
'Breathing fresh air into training', Anat Arkin in *People Management,* 27 July, 1995
'OMD holds a mirror up to office life', Andy Dickson in *Financial Training Review,* August 1995
'Putting a value on fresh air', Fiona Moore in *Training (Personnel Today Magazine),* October 1995
'Partnership teams solve problems', *Management Training,* November/ December 1995
'The future of development training', Gina Channel in *Human Resources,* January/February 1996
'Keep on trucking', Mary Arigho in *Personnel Today,* 10 April, 1996
'Why managers go wild about the outdoor life', Abigail Montrose in *Financial Director,* April 1996
'Take a fresh look at work', Stephanie Sparrow in *Training (Personnel Today Magazine),* April 1996

Index